THE *Ivy House*
RESTAURANT
Williston, Florida

1

ISBN-13: 978-0-9763062-0-7

Publisher: Florida Media Inc

999 Douglas Avenue Suite 3301
Altamonte Springs, Florida 32714

Phone: 407-816-9596
Fax: 407-816-9373
www.floridamagazine.com

Printed in the United States of America

Library of Congress Cataloging-in-Publication Data

Hale, Marjorie
Gracefully Southern
ISBN-13: 978-0-9763062-0-7

By *Marjorie Hale*

Our Desire

We strive to maintain the
homemade quality of our food.

OUR FAITH IN GOD,
hard long hours, in addition to the
WONDERFUL CUSTOMERS
we have, make it possible.

How else could we succeed
in a small country town,
on a side street, if God did not

BLESS US WITH WONDERFUL,
sweet customers who He sends to us.

BAKED
Krispy Chicken

8 boneless chicken breasts
1 stick butter, melted
1-2 cups Rice Krispies
Salt and pepper to taste

- **Dip chicken in the melted butter; then roll in crushed Rice Krispies.**

- Bake in a shallow baking pan at 325° - 350°
  for 20-25 minutes or until golden brown.

OUR SIGNATURE RECIPE

My sister Dot gave me this recipe.
She was a counselor/teacher in Pensacola, Fl.
My sister hated to cook, but this was so simple
and good that she could not resist.

THIS RECIPE IS SO SIMPLE,
BUT SO GOOD.
IT IS TRULY AN
IVY HOUSE FAVORITE
AND ONE WHICH IS REQUESTED
FOR SO MANY SPECIAL OCCASIONS.

SECRET FAMILY RECIPE
Southern Pork Chops

6

This is a favorite at the Ivy House.
It is a secret we are not willing to give away just yet.
We invite you to come see why this is an Ivy House Favorite.
Served Daily

Southern Fried Shrimp
SECRET FAMILY RECIPE

9

SECRET FAMILY RECIPE

Fried Green Tomatoes

Ivy House

OUR SIGNATURE
Coconut Dream Cake

11

Recipe on page 191

OUR SIGNATURE
Cherry Torte

12

Recipe on page 218

OUR SIGNATURE

Blueberry Torte

13

Recipe on page 218

OUR SIGNATURE
Lemon Chiffon Cake

14

Recipe on page 183

OUR SIGNATURE
German Chocolate LAYERED CAKE

15

Recipe on page 195

Recipe on page 184

Sincere Thanks

FOR YOUR SUPPORT, FAITHFULNESS AND PRAYERS
TOWARDS THE COOKBOOK.

Leslie Paramore
Charles & Diane Webb
Cynthia McFarland
Judy Welbourn
Doug Cifers

Diane Pierce
Elaine & Carlos Ramerez
Brother Chester & Beverly Clarke
Robert Beauchamp
Wendy Reynolds
George and Libby Lane

DESIGN AND LAYOUT BY:
Wendy Reynolds

PHOTOGRAPHY BY:
ELEMENTS DESIGN STUDIO
Steve & Wendy Reynolds

www.edsphoto.net

PRINTING & PUBLISHING BY:

FLORIDA MEDIA, INC.

www.floridamagazine.com

FOR THE MANY ARTICLES THAT HAVE BEEN
WRITTEN IN YOUR MAGAZINES AND NEWSPAPERS
ON OUR WILLISTON LOCATION:

Florida Monthly
Crystal River Paper
Senior Times Magazine
Florida Secrets
Ocala Style Magazine

Florida Trend Magazine
Williston Pioneer Sun News
Channel 20 - Paige Beck, Gainesville
Gainesville Sun
Ocala Star Banner

My Kitchen

I PREHEAT A MEMORY
I FOLD IN OLD FRIENDS WITH NEW
I FRY UP NEW IDEAS
I BAKE A GOOD LAUGH
I COOK UP A FEW NEW DREAMS
I SERVE UP MANY BLESSINGS

WHAT'S IN YOUR KITCHEN?

To our
Mother, Grandmother & Great-Grandmother

To: Our Mother, Grandmother & Great-Grandmother (MiMi)

What an inspiration you are to all of us. You have been our family rock with your prayers, kind understanding, your soft-spoken words of wisdom, and most of all, your unconditional love. WE ARE SO PROUD OF YOUR ACCOMPLISHMENTS.

Something that has always been a dream, you made a reality, through hard work and faith in God that He would carry you through, and that, He has done. It will be such a joy to know that a little bit of your life and a lot of your wonderful food will bless many other families the same way it has blessed ours.

There is nothing more special than gathering around a dining table as family, reminiscing of special times, and enjoying a wonderfully home-cooked meal straight from the heart. KNOWING THAT YOU WILL BE A PART OF THAT IS SO AMAZING!

God said He would send down the angels, but we live among one every day. You are truly an angel, not only to your family, but to many friends as well. You have touched so many lives with your kind words of encouragement and, of course, your delicious food that you prepare so gracefully.

A true lady is what you are, always finding a kind word to say about someone. The passion that you have for cooking, we hope will carry on for many generations.
WE ARE SO BLESSED TO HAVE YOU IN OUR LIVES.

We love you!

Your Beloved Family

Contents

APPETIZERS, PARTY FOODS & BEVERAGES
Page 21-44

BREAKFAST & BRUNCH
Page 45-58

SOUPS, SALADS & SALAD DRESSINGS
Page 59-83

VEGETABLES, STARCHES & PASTA
Page 84-111

MAIN DISHES, MEAT, POULTRY & SEAFOOD
Page 130-162

SAUCES
Page 163-169

BREADS & ROLLS
Page 170-179

DESSERTS
Page 180-235

Appetizers, Party Foods & Beverages

Chicken Balls

3 cups chicken, boiled
3 ounces cream cheese
3 tablespoons of mayonaise
2 tablespoons orange marmalade
3 tablespoons green onions, minced
3 tablespoons celery, minced
1 teaspoons curry powder (optional)
Salt and pepper to taste
1 cup toasted almonds, crushed - sliced almonds

- **Boil chicken until tender, drain and chop.**
- Cream the cheese and mayonaise, mix with the orange marmalade, green onions, celery, curry powder, salt and pepper.
- **Fold in chicken and mix well.**
- Roll mixture into bite-size balls, and then roll in toasted crushed almonds.

These are delicious for any special occasion.
This is Susan Webb and Evelyn's favorite and is sure to be a hit with

YOUR FAMILY AND FRIENDS AS WELL.

Green Olive Puffs

Yield: 4 dozen

1/2 cup butter
2 cups cheddar cheese, finely shredded
1 1/4 cups plain flour
1 teaspoon paprika
48 stuffed green olives

- **Mix butter, cheese, flour and paprika until a dough forms.**

- Shape into a small ball and refrigerate 15-20 minutes.

- **Meanwhile, drain olives and allow to dry.**

- With floured hands, mold 1/2 teaspoon dough around each dry olive.

- **Chill overnight.**

- When ready to use, bake in a preheated oven at 400° for 10-12 minutes until lightly browned.

OLIVE PUFFS

23

Party Cheese Ring

1 pound mixed cheddar cheese, shredded
8 ounces cream cheese
3/4 cup mayonnaise
1 medium onion, finely chopped
1 cloves garlic, minced
1/2 teaspoon hot sauce (I prefer Louisiana)
1/2 cup pecans or almonds, toasted and chopped, set aside for garnish
1 tablespoon of worcestershire

- **In a mixer cream the cream cheese and mayonaise together first, then add all other ingredients except nuts and blend well.**
- Shape into a ball.
- **Generously sprinkle with nuts.**
- Serve with crackers or toasted rounds.

PARTY CHEESE RING

Tip:

To add a special touch, make a hole in the middle of the ball and fill with your favorite marmalade. Oh, so good! For the holidays, you can shape into a pinecone, cover with roasted pecan halves or almonds and add a sprig of greenery at the top. Customers just love this cheese spread.

WE SERVE IT AT THE RESTAURANT FOR AN APPETIZER WITH CRACKERS.

MiMi's Chicken Salad

Yield: 6 servings

6 chicken breasts, cooked
1/2 cup celery, finely chopped
1/2 cup mayonnaise
1/4 cup sliced almonds, toasted
Salt and pepper to taste
Grapes, strawberries, or cantaloupe for garnish

- **Boil chicken until tender; drain and chop.**
- Add celery, mayonnaise, and almonds.
- **Gently fold all ingredients together.**
- Serve on your favorite bread, croissant or lettuce leaf.
- **Garnish with grapes, strawberries, or cantaloupe.**

CHICKEN SALAD

CHICKEN SALAD

Tip:

THIS CHICKEN SALAD IS SO VERSATILE AND ALWAYS WELL RECEIVED.
DON'T FORGET TO SAVE YOUR CHICKEN BROTH TO PUT IN YOUR
HOMEMADE SOUPS OR GREEN STRING BEANS.

I ALWAYS SAY, IT'S LIKE GOLD, NEVER THROW IT OUT.

Baked Sweet Onion Dip

3 large onions, coarsely chopped
2 tbsp. sugar
2 tbsp. butter
2 tbsp. olive oil
2 cups Swiss cheese, shredded
2 cups mayonnaise
1 (8 oz.) can water chestnuts, drained and chopped
1/4 cup white grape juice- my substitution for white wine
1 clove garlic, minced
1/2 teaspoon hot sauce

- **Melt butter and add olive oil in a large skillet over medium-high heat.**

- Add the onion and sauté 10 minutes or until tender.

- **Stir together all ingredients until mixed well and pour into 9 x13 baking dish.**

- Bake at 375° for 25 minutes.

- **Let stand for a few minutes before serving with your favorite chips, crackers, or tortillas.**

BAKED SWEET
ONION DIP

EBBIE'S *Meat Dip*

2 pounds ground sirloin beef
1 pound Velveeta cheese, cubed
1 can Rotel mild tomatoes (spice it up with the "hot" Rotel tomatoes)

- **Brown meat and drain well.**
- In a medium sauce pan, combine the meat, cheese and tomatoes.
- **Cook over medium heat until cheese is melted, stirring regularly.**
- Do not let mixture boil.
- **Serve with nacho or tortilla chips.**

MEAT DIP

Party Meatballs

2 pounds ground sirloin beef
2 eggs
1 sleeve Saltine crackers, finely crushed
1 large onion, finely chopped
1/2 cup canned cream (evaporated milk)
1/2 cup water

- **Mix all ingredients and roll into bite-size meatballs.**
- Place in a 9 x 13 baking dish.
- **Bake in a preheated 350° oven for 30 minutes.**
- Drain well.
- **Add meatballs to the sauce (see recipe below).**
- Simmer an additional 10 minutes.

SAUCE

1 (10 oz.) jar grape jelly
1 small bottle chili sauce

- **Mix the jelly and chili sauce in a pan and heat over medium heat until melted.**
- Add meatballs and simmer for 10 minutes.

Tip:

Depending on your personal taste, you may substitute party sausage in the recipe. These meatballs are also great without the sauce to add to your favorite spaghetti sauce.

Cream Cheese & Pepper Jelly

8 ounces cream cheese
1 (6 oz.) jar pepper jelly

- **Place the block of cream cheese on a serving dish.**
- Spread jelly over the cheese to cover.
- **Serve with an array of your favorite crackers.**

Quick and easy,
BUT A HIT EVERY TIME!

SIMPLY DELICIOUS.

WE TRY TO USE JELLY THAT GOES WITH THE COLOR OF THE SEASON.
GARNISH WITH A MINT LEAF OR TWO, OR WITH OUR FAVORITE... IVY LEAVES.
REMEMBER, THE SERVING DISH MAKES A STATEMENT TOO.

Waica's Favorite
CREAM CHEESE & HAM PINWHEELS

6 slices boiled ham
3 ounces cream cheese
2 tablespoons mayonnaise
6 green spring onions

- **Mix cream cheese and mayonnaise until blended and of spreading consistency.**
- Spread a small amount on one slice of ham.
- **Place one onion on the edge of the ham and roll up.**
- Repeat with the remaining slices of ham.
- **Refrigerate rolls 30 minutes or longer.**
- Before serving, slice each roll into six to eight pieces.
- **Serve on platter.**

THIS RECIPE IS SO **DELICIOUS** MADE WITH FRESH ASPARAGUS SPEARS OR PICKLED OKRA INSTEAD OF THE GREEN ONION.

Brie & Bread

1 round loaf bread
1 wedge Brie

- **Scoop out the center of the bread.**
- Remove white skin from the Brie and cut into chunks.
- **Place Brie chunks into center of bread.**
- Bake in a 350° oven until cheese is soft and of dipping consistency.
- **Tear remaining bread into chunks.**
- To serve, place the warm Brie and bread round on platter with chunks piled around it.

BRIE & BREAD

For fall, ADD ORANGE MARMALADE AND
FRESH CRANBERRIES TO THE CENTER, AS WELL AS BRIE.

For Christmas, ADD FRESH CRANBERRIES AND MINT JELLY.
ADD OUR FAVORITE PESTO SAUCE (PAGE 169) TO THE CENTER FOR
A DIFFERENT TASTE. YUM, YUM!

Hearty Hot Beef Dip

2 (8 oz.) packages cream cheese
1 pint sour cream
1 (4.5 oz.) jar dried beef

- **Rinse dried beef in water to remove excess salt.**
- Chop the beef.
- **Mix all ingredients together and warm thoroughly over medium heat, stirring frequently.**
- You may add a little spring onion for flavor or garnish.
- **Serve with wavy potato chips or fresh raw vegetables.**

Bacon Water Chestnuts

16 slices bacon, cut into halves
1 (10 oz.) can water chestnuts, drained and cut into halves
1/2 cup brown sugar
1/2 cup soy sauce
1/4 teaspoon ginger

- **Mix the brown sugar, soy sauce and ginger in a bowl.**
- Add the chestnuts and soak 20–30 minutes.
- **Wrap each chestnut with bacon and seal with a toothpick.**
- Place chestnuts in a baking dish and bake 350° - 375° until bacon is browned.

Easy Artichoke Dip

Yield: 3 1/2 cups

1 (12 oz.) can artichokes, drained and broken into pieces
1 cup parmesan cheese, grated
1/2 cup mayonnaise
1/8 teaspoon garlic, minced

- **Mix all ingredients and spoon into a sprayed one quart baking dish.**
- Bake 15 minutes at 350°.
- **Serve warm with your favorite chips or crackers.**

ARTICHOKE DIP

THIS DIP PRESENTS WELL WHEN BAKED IN
A NICE BAKING DISH OR ONE THAT
CAN BE PLACED IN A PRETTY HOLDER.
TO ADD A MEXICAN FLARE TO YOUR DIP,
TRY ADDING A 4 OZ. CAN OF CHOPPED GREEN CHILES.

Old-Fashioned Homemade Pimento Cheese

1 pound cheddar cheese, shredded
1/2 cup mayonnaise (or to taste)
1 small jar pimentos, drained

- **Combine all ingredients and chill.**
- When ready to serve, make sandwiches with your favorite kind of bread.

FOR A SPECIAL TREAT, TRY YOUR PIMENTO SANDWICH GRILLED.
THIS PIMENTO CHEESE MIXTURE IS ALSO DELICIOUS STUFFED IN CELERY
AND SO ATTRACTIVE SERVED ON A PRETTY PLATTER OR CUT GLASS PLATE.

Cooked Pimento & Cheese

1 pound cheddar cheese, shredded
1 (12 oz.) canned cream (evaporated milk)
1 medium jar pimentos, drained

- **Mix all ingredients in a sauce pan and cook over low heat.**
- Stir until mixture is well blended.
- **Cool and serve on your choice of bread.**

THIS IS TRULY AN "OLDIE GOLDIE" FAVORITE,
ONE THAT WE GET MANY REQUESTS FOR.

FLOWER SANDWICHES – *Calla Lily*

24 slices white bread
1 (8 oz.) package cream cheese, softened
2 tablespoons orange marmalade
1 (2 oz.) package slivered almonds
2 – 3 drops yellow food coloring

- **Roll each slice of bread with a rolling pin.**
- Cut with a 2 1/2 inch cutter and set aside.
- **Combine cream cheese and marmalade and chill slightly.**
- Spread about 1 1/2 teaspoon of mixture on bread rounds
- **Fold bread in half and press together at the bottom end to form a flower.**
- Shake slivered almonds in the yellow food coloring in a jar to get them evenly colored.
- **Put an almond in the top end to look like a flower's stamen.**

CALLA LILY

THESE PARTY SANDWICHES ARE SO DAINTY & DELICIOUS
AND ARE SO PRETTY TO SERVE AT A SPECIAL EVENT,
WEDDING RECEPTION OR BRIDAL LUNCHEON.

Old-Fashioned Angel Eggs

1 dozen eggs, boiled
1 cup mayonnaise
1/3 cup sweet pickle relish
1/3 cup green olives, finely chopped
Salt and pepper, to taste
Paprika, for garnish

- **Boil eggs.**
- Cool, peel, and split eggs into halves.
- **Mix egg yolks, mayonnaise, relish, green olives, salt and pepper.**
- Stuff each egg white with half the mixture.
- **Sprinkle with paprika.**

Try these favorites with fresh cooked bacon crumbles sprinkled on top.
A SPECIAL TREAT FOR SURE!
This recipe is the original deviled eggs, but MiMi just refuses
to call them deviled eggs, much less, eat them.

Another option is to leave out the sweet pickle relish and green olives.
THEY ARE STILL GREAT.

My grandchildren like it this way better,
but I tell them when they get older, their taste buds will change
and they will probably love it with relish and olives.

Our Favorite Coffee Punch

1 gallon strong brewed coffee, well chilled
1 (16 oz.) can chocolate syrup to taste, optional
1/2 gallon vanilla ice cream
1 (12 oz.) canned cream (evaporated milk)
1 cup sugar

- **Mix the chilled coffee, chocolate syrup, sugar and evaporated milk.**

- Cut the ice cream into small pieces and place in a punch bowl.

- **Pour the coffee mixture over the ice cream and stir until slightly blended.**

- Garnish with cool whip or shaved chocolate or sprinkle with cinnamon.

MY GRANDDAUGHTER, ALESHA,
relishes this punch. Even people who do not drink coffee love it.

Adding vanilla ice cream and, of course,
canned cream, really mellows this punch so that
THE FLAVOR OF THE COFFEE IS VERY LIGHT.

For those who don't drink coffee, be careful,
YOU MIGHT GET HOOKED!

GREAT *Raspberry Mix* USES

Regular and Sugar Free

- **Add Sprite or ginger ale or club soda. So refreshing!**
- Stir into cool whip for a fruit dip. Yummy!
- **Pour over vanilla ice cream or frozen yogurt.**
- Add to our wedding punch recipe.
- **Pour over ice and blend for a raspberry slushy.**
- Add a splash to your favorite lemonade or plain ice water.
- **Add just the amount of syrup for your tasting (a little goes a long way.)**

RASPBERRY MIX

Raspberry Iced Tea
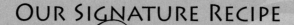

1 box Bigelow raspberry tea bags
3/4 gallon of water
4 oz. Southern Raspberry Mix (sold at The Ivy House)
3/4 cup sugar
1 cup fresh lemon juice
4 scoops of Country Time lemonade mix

- **Bring water to a boil and add tea bags.**
- Remove from heat and allow to steep approximately 30 minutes (longer will not adversely affect the brew).
- **Remove the bags and add the remaining four ingredients.**
- Stir until well mixed and sugar is dissolved.
- **Adjust sugar to your taste. (My Ann makes it sweet!!)**
- **Makes close to 1 gallon.**

This recipe was created by my first born, Ann.
THIS IS A SIGNATURE DRINK IN OUR RESTAURANT.

NO ONE CAN MAKE IT LIKE MY ANN
BECAUSE IT IS HOMEMADE, NOT STORE BOUGHT.

Don't forget to check out the great recipes
on the Ivy House Southern Raspberry Mix bottles.

Old-Fashioned Red Punch

Yield: 1 gallon

1 large package strawberry Kool-aid with sugar added
1 large can pineapple juice
1 cup sugar
1 small bottle lemon juice concentrate
Water, enough to bring the mixture to one gallon
1 large bottle ginger ale, chilled

- **Mix all ingredients except ginger ale in large container.**
- Stir until sugar is dissolved.
- **Refrigerate until well chilled.**
- Serve with ice or freeze an ice ring from a little of the punch and float it in the bowl when ready to serve.
- **Pour ginger ale over mixture and ice for a bubble effect.**

THIS IS A PRETTY PUNCH

to use for Valentine's Day, Christmas, or your 4th of July celebration. It is best when made the day before, allowing the flavors to blend.

"FALL YA'LL PUNCH"

Substitute the strawberry Kool-aid with orange Kool-aid.

"SUMMERTIME SPLASH PUNCH"

Substitute the strawberry Kool-aid with lemon Kool-aid and add a splash of our Southern Raspberry mix.

Wedding Punch

Yield: 28 - 4 oz. cups

1 bottle (48 ounces) white grape juice
1 2-liter ginger ale
1 ice ring

- **Chill the grape juice and the ginger ale.**
- Prepare an ice ring or cubed or crushed ice.
- **When ready to serve, pour the two ingredients into a punch bowl over the ice ring.**

THIS PUNCH IS ABSOLUTELY DELICIOUS SERVED PLAIN,
or you can dress it up by adding small scoops of vanilla ice cream, stirring to blend.

ALSO, YOU CAN STIR IN FRESH SEASONAL FRUITS,
like blueberries, raspberries, diced peaches, strawberries and mandarin oranges.
With leftover punch, add yogurt and blend for a zesty smoothie.

Morning Punch

Yield: 4 servings

1 cup orange juice
1 banana
1/2 cup strawberries
1 cup ice cubes
1 tablespoon honey
1/2 cup pineapple, crushed

- **Mix all ingredients together in a blender.**
- Serve immediately in footed glasses.
- **Top off with a mint leaf and a wedge of fruit.**

MORNING PUNCH

WE HAVE SERVED THIS MORNING PUNCH MANY TIMES TO OUR FORMER BED & BREAKFAST GUESTS. THIS WOULD ALSO BE GREAT FOR BRUNCHES.

Special Occasion Punch

Yields 60 - 8oz servings

3 gallons orange juice
1 large can pineapple juice
1 can cream de cocoa
1/2 bottle grenadine

- **Mix all ingredients in a large container.**
- Chill well.
- **Serve in a punch bowl.**

THIS IS A PUNCH THAT OUR FAMILY HAS ENJOYED
AT OUR ANNUAL SUMMER VACATION IN MARCO ISLAND.

IT'S SUCH A GREAT SPLASH OF CITRUS ON A
HOT SUMMER DAY.

Piña Colada Punch

1 large can pineapple juice
1 (15 oz.) can cream of coconut
1 2-liter Sprite or 7-Up
Cherry Kool-Aid

- **Mix pineapple juice and cream of coconut.**
- Add just enough of the cherry Kool-Aid to obtain the desired shade of pink.
- **Pour 1/3 of mixture into a mold and freeze.**
- When ready to serve, put the ice ring in a punch bowl, add punch mixture and the Sprite or 7-Up. (Do not substitute ginger ale or other beverage as it will change the pretty color.)

PIÑA COLADA PUNCH

Breakfast & Brunch

Fruit Compote

Sliced bananas
Frozen sweet strawberries, thawed
Canned cream (evaporated milk)

- **Place sliced bananas in small footed dessert dishes, about 1 cup size.**

- Spoon about 4 teaspoons of frozen strawberries and juice over bananas.

- **Pour 1/3 cup chilled evaporated canned milk over fruit.**

- Put a paper doily on a small plate and place the footed dish on the top before serving.

THIS IS ONE OF THOSE SIMPLE BUT DELICIOUS DISHES!
IT'S A GREAT START TO A FULL COUNTRY BREAKFAST.

Sour Cream Pancakes

Yield: 4-6 pancakes

1 cup self-rising flour
1 cup sour cream
1 tablespoon sugar
4 large eggs, well beaten

- **Mix flour, sour cream, sugar, and eggs until lightly blended.**
- Spoon batter onto lightly greased griddle or skillet and brown on each side.
- **Serve with blueberries and cool whip or with your favorite syrup.**

SOUR CREAM PANCAKES

THE CHARM OF THE
OLE' SOUTH SOUTHERN HOSPITALITY
IS FADING OUT FASTER THAN WE KNOW.

IT IS OUR DESIRE FOR PEOPLE TO EXPERIENCE THIS
IN THEIR HOMES AND LIVES EVERY DAY.

Velvety Waffles

Yields: 8 servings

2 cups self-rising flour
1 tablespoon sugar
3 eggs, slightly beaten
1/2 cup vegetable oil
1/2 teaspoon vanilla flavoring
1 3/4 cups milk or buttermilk (add a pinch of baking soda if using buttermilk)

- **Sift flour and sugar in mixing bowl.**
- Combine the milk, eggs and oil.
- **Add to the flour mixture fold in gently.**
- Spoon batter into pre-heated waffle iron and cook until done.
- **Butter each waffle and stack on serving platter.**
- Serve with warm syrup.

This batter may also be prepared as pancakes.
Just pour onto heated (325°) greased griddle and allow to bubble.
Turn and brown on the other side.

VERY GOOD EITHER WAY.

Ivy House Country French Toast

Yield: 1 serving

1 kaiser bun or french bread
1 heaping tablespoon cream cheese
1 tablespoon jelly or jam
1 egg, beaten
1/2 cup milk
1 teaspoon butter

- **Turn kaiser buns inside out and spread cream cheese on one piece of the bread and spread jelly or jam on the other.**

- Press together.

- **Lightly spread the butter on both sides of the "sandwich."**

- Mix beaten egg and milk and dip the bun, turning to coat all sides with the mixture.

- **Transfer to a medium hot griddle and toast until golden brown on both sides.**

- Sprinkle with confectioners sugar (for sure).

- **Garnish with a mint leaf and seasonal favorite fruit.**

- Drizzle with syrup.

Eggs & Sausage Morning Casserole

Yield: 12 servings

6 slices white bread
1 pound hot sausage
1 teaspoon dry mustard
5 eggs
2 1/4 cups milk
1 1/2 cups shredded cheese
1 teaspoon salt
Dash of Tabasco
1/2 stick butter

- **Cook and crumble sausage; drain fat.**
- Cut crust off bread, then butter and cube it.
- **Place bread in a 9 x 13 casserole dish.**
- Sprinkle with sausage.
- **Mix together eggs, mustard, milk, salt and Tabasco.**
- Pour over the bread and sausage.
- **Top with cheese.**
- Refrigerate overnight. Bake at 350° for 35-40 minutes.

Banana Raisin French Toast

Yield: 4 servings

8 slices raisin bread
2 medium bananas, cut in 1/4 inch slices
1 cup milk
4 ounces cream cheese, softened
3 eggs
1/3 cup sugar
3 tablespoons flour
2 teaspoons vanilla
Powdered sugar, optional

- **Place four slices of the raisin bread in a single layer in a buttered 9 x 9 casserole dish.**
- Top with bananas and the remaining four slices of the bread.
- **Combine the milk, cream cheese, eggs, sugar, flour and vanilla in a blender.**
- Blend until smooth.
- **Pour over the raisin bread and let stand for five minutes.**
- Bake in a 350° oven for 40-45 minutes, or until set and top is brown.
- **Let stand 10 minutes.**
- Cut into diagonal halves and remove with a spatula.
- **Dust each half with powdered sugar if desired and serve plain or with syrup on the side.**

This may be prepared ahead and refrigerated overnight.
If so, merely add approximately 10 minutes to the baking time.

MiMi's Breakfast Bread

2 cans refrigerated flaky biscuits, split each biscuit in half
1 cup sugar
1 tablespoon apple pie spice
1 stick butter, melted
1 cup brown sugar
1 (8 oz.) package cream cheese
1 cup grape jelly

- **Place small amount of the cream cheese and jelly on each biscuit half and fold over, pinching together slightly.**
- Place in a 9 x 13 baking dish.
- **Mix sugars, spice, and butter and pour mixture over biscuits.**
- Bake in a preheated 350° oven until golden brown.
- **Serve warm.**

THIS RECIPE IS SO SIMPLE,
BUT SO GOOD.
IT'S ONE OF WAICA'S FAVORITES.
QUICK, EASY & DELICIOUS!

Cheese Grits

Yield: 4-6 servings

1 cup quick cooking grits
3 cups water
1 cup milk
1 stick butter
1 cup cheddar cheese, shredded
1 teaspoon salt

- **Combine first four ingredients in a large sauce pan and bring to a boil.**
- Cook on medium heat for 20-30 minutes, stirring occasionally.
- **Add cheese and salt; stir well until cheese is melted.**
- Serve hot.

I have made cheese grits all my life. I can remember my nephew
(Bill Moore) screaming in his high chair, I want cheese grits!
SO, EVERY TIME HE COMES TO VISIT, YES, WE HAVE CHEESE GRITS.

IN PETITE MUFFIN PANS

- **For a different twist on this delicious recipe, add one small can of chopped chiles to the cheese grits and spoon in sprayed, miniature muffin pan.**
- Bake in preheated 350° oven for 20 minutes or until golden brown.

One of our fine Williston men, Ronnie Thomas, said he could have eaten a bushel
of these tasty treats. He really enjoyed them, and I know you will, too.
We do a lot of catering for his former wife, Becky Thomas Ray, and we always have to fix these.
Their daughter, sweet Justa, says it's a must on the menu. She loves them like her father did.

SAUSAGE GRAVY

Sausage Gravy

Yield: 4-6 servings

1 pound bulk pork sausage
1 (3 oz.) package cream cheese, softened
1/4 teaspoon salt
1 can cream of mushroom soup
1 can canned cream (evaporated milk)
1 tablespoon self-rising flour

- **In a heavy skillet, brown sausage.**
- Drain excess grease.
- **Mix together cream cheese, salt , mushroom soup, canned cream and flour.**
- Add to the sausage mixture and cook on medium heat for 15 minutes.
- **Serve hot over biscuit halves or cheese grits.**

Christmas Morning
"The Hale House"
Sausage Gravy

This is served for our family
CHRISTMAS MORNING BREAKFAST EVERY YEAR.

It's great served over my biscuits. It truly melts in your mouth.
Christmas wouldn't be the same without it.

Every Christmas morning our family gathers around the
kitchen island waiting in line for a turn to
get their spoonful of this wonderful sausage gravy.

No one could make it like "Big Joe," Micala and Lil' Joe's daddy.
HE MADE IT TO PERFECTION.
Everyone has their own dish to add to the morning breakfast.
I make my wonderful eggs. I learned to cook 28 eggs at a time
in a sheet pan with butter. Best fried eggs ever, sunny side up!

Michael or Papa squeezes out the fresh orange juice. Art cooks his famous
creamy grits, Waica brings her praline french toast, and then
I make my knuckle biscuits for that good ole' gravy.

Ann makes her homemade country fried potatoes,
and Myra brings her homemade cinnamon rolls, but
I told Waica that we had to come up with
something Evelyn did and she laughed and then said,
"She does coordinate the Christmas paper goods."
The gathering of this Christmas breakfast is dear to my heart,
memories our family will cherish forever.
I ALWAYS SAY, "WE'RE MAKING MEMORIES!"

MiMi's Favorite Quiche
"THE BEST"

Yield: 8 slices

1 pie crust, ready-made
2 eggs
1/2 cup canned cream (evaporated milk)
1/2 cup mayonnaise
1 cup shredded cheddar cheese
1 cup shredded mozzarella cheese

- **Unroll pie crust into a 9" pie plate.**
- Mix all ingredients and pour into the unbaked crust.
- **Bake in preheated oven at 350° for 30-40 minutes.**
- Allow to stand 15 minutes before cutting and serving.

Everyone tells me my recipe is the best they have ever eaten.
It's not your traditional eggy quiche. It's creamy and light. The secret is the mayonnaise.

This quiche is delicious served plain, but can be very versatile, depending on your taste and the occasion.
Try adding in one of the following ingredients for a quiche your guests are sure to rave about:
chopped broccoli, chopped asparagus, mushrooms, chopped ham, crumbled sausage,
or 1/2 cup sautéed chopped onion, bacon and spinach.

TIP: Saute' mushrooms, onion and bacon before adding to quiche mixture.

Onion, Tomato & Basil Quiche

Yield: 2 pies

2 pie crusts, refrigerated
1 onion, sliced into thin 1/2" circles
2 cups shredded white cheddar cheese
3 ripe tomatoes, sliced 1/2" thick
4 tablespoons fresh basil, coarsely chopped
5 eggs, lightly beaten and add 1/2 cup mayonaise to eggs
2 cups heavy cream
Salt and pepper

- **Spray pie pans and fit crust in each.**
- Place parchment paper over pastries and weight with dry beans or rice.
- **Bake 12-15 minutes at 350°.**
- Remove parchment and weights and continue to bake for approximately eight more minutes.
- **Remove from oven and set aside.**
- **Sauté onions with a pinch of salt and pepper, cool.**
- Layer the ingredients in pie crust as follows: onion, cheese, tomato, basil.
- **Combine eggs, mayonaise , heavy cream and set aside.**
- Pour cream mixture over layers.
- Bake at 350° for 25-30 minutes.

Lemon Cranberry Muffins

Yield: 20-22 muffins

3 3/4 cups self-rising flour
3 tablespoons grated lemon peel
1 1/2 cups sugar
1/2 cup vegetable oil
1 egg
1 cup sour cream
1 cup fresh cranberries, chopped

- **Mix flour, lemon peel, and sugar; set aside.**
- Mix oil, egg and sour cream; and add to the dry ingredients; stir gently.
- **Fold in cranberries and spoon into greased muffin tin, filling each 2/3 full.**
- Bake at 350° for 15-20 minutes until golden brown.

Sometimes if I do not have fresh cranberries, I use other fruits, like peaches, strawberries, blueberries, or mandarin oranges drained. All are good choices.

You can fill the muffin tin with mixture to the rim for a high muffin top.

ENJOY!

Soups, Salads & Dressings

TOMATO SOUP

Creamy Tomato Soup

1 can diced tomatoes- processed until smooth
1 can canned cream (evaporated milk) add 2 tablespoons of self-rising flour, blend until smooth
Fresh chopped basil, to taste
Salt and pepper, to taste
Crisp crumbled bacon, optional

- **Mix tomatoes, canned cream, basil, flour, salt and pepper.**
- Cook over medium heat until thoroughly heated.
- **Serve in bowls and sprinkle with bacon.**

Baked Potato Soup

4 chopped baked potatoes, skin and all
1 stick butter
2/3 cup all-purpose flour
1 tablespoon chives
1 cup sour cream
4 cups whole milk
Crisp, crumbled bacon, optional
Salt and pepper, to taste

- **Melt butter in a sauce pan.**
- Stir in the flour and blend until smooth.
- **Gradually add the milk, stirring gradually.**
- Cook until thickened.
- **Stir in the sour cream and chives, then add the potatoes and heat thoroughly.**
- Add more milk, if needed, for a creamy consistency.
- **Spoon into bowls or cups, garnish with crisp, crumbled bacon, and serve.**

BAKED POTATO
SOUP

Collard Green Soup

1 bag frozen chopped collard greens
1 pound ham hocks
Salt and pepper to taste
2 large sweet potatoes, baked and cut into cubes
1 can great northern beans, drained
1 large onion, coarsely chopped
1 pound smoked sausage, thinly sliced and sautéed until browned
1 cup canned cream (evaporated milk)

- **Put greens, ham, salt, pepper and onion in a large pot.**
- Add enough water to cover, bring to a boil.
- **Cook on medium for one hour.**
- Add the beans and sausage and simmer another 30 minutes.
- **During the last 15 minutes of cooking, fold in the sweet potatoes.**

COLLARD
GREEN SOUP

MAKE MY GOOD
BUTTERMILK CORNBREAD,
baked in your black iron skillet; then enjoy this good hearty supper.
You won't believe the amount of flavor in the soup.

NEW ENGLAND *Clam Chowder*

Yield: 6 servings

1/2 cup onion, chopped
1 slice bacon, cut into small pieces
2 (8 oz.) cans minced clams, drained (reserved liquid)
1/2 cup potato, finely chopped
Salt and pepper to taste
1 cup whole milk
1 cup canned cream (evaporated milk)

- **Cook and stir the onion and bacon in sauce pan until onion is tender and bacon is crisp.**
- Add enough water to the reserved clam liquid to measure 1 cup.
- **Stir in clams and liquid, chopped potato, salt and pepper into the onion mixture.**
- Heat to boiling; cover and simmer until potatoes are done, about 15 minutes.
- **Add milk and cream; heat thoroughly, stirring frequently.**
- Serve hot.

French Onion Soup

1/4 cup butter
4 large onions, halved and thinly sliced
1 teaspoon sugar
1 tablespoon all-purpose flour
3 (10.5 oz.) cans beef consomme'
1 1/4 cups of water
1/4 cup grape juice, my substitution for white wine
1 slice of French bread toasted, about 1 inch thick
4 slices Provolone cheese

- **Melt butter over medium high heat.**
- Add onions and stir to coat onions well.
- **Cover and cook eight minutes, stirring occasionally.**
- Uncover, add the sugar and continue cooking for approximately six minutes, stirring until onions are slightly golden brown.
- **Blend in the flour and cook another minute; then add the beef consommae', water and grape juice, stirring to mix well.**
- **Cover and simmer 5 minutes.**
- Place four 2-cup ovenproof bowls on a baking sheet and add toasted French bread to each bowl.
- **Evenly divide soup among bowls, topping each with a slice of cheese.**
- Broil three minutes or until cheese melts.
- **Serve hot.**

THIS IS SIMPLY DELICIOUS AND TASTES LIKE IT COMES STRAIGHT FROM MY

FRENCH COUNTRY KITCHEN!

Oyster Stew

1/4 cup butter
1 pint oyster, drained (reserve the liquid)
2 cups milk
1/2 cup liquid from the oysters
Salt and pepper to taste
Dash of cayenne pepper
Dash of worcestershire sauce
Paprika to taste
Oyster crackers, of course

- **Heat butter in medium skillet until melted.**
- Add oysters.
- **Cook and stir over low heat just until edges curl.**
- Heat milk, cream and oyster liquid in a 2 quart saucepan.
- **Stir in salt, cayenne pepper, worcestershire sauce and oysters.**
- Serve with oyster crackers.

I had never eaten oyster stew before, until Freddie and I went
to Dan and Betty Whitehurst's home for supper.
He was making oyster stew and fried home-grown quail
that was raised on his family farm.

Dan gave me a bowl of stew. I was very hesitant to try it, but I did.
Dan asked if I wanted another bowl full, and I had to say,
"No, I'll wait for the quail."
The stew was good, but oysters are not my favorite.
But, oh, how my husband Freddie loved it. The recipe is a good one.

I HOPE YOU ENJOY IT AS MUCH AS FREDDIE.

Brunswick Stew

Yield: 8-10 servings

3 center cut pork chops
3 pounds chicken, cut into bite-size pieces
4 cups water
Salt and pepper to taste
2 (16 oz.) cans diced tomatoes
1 (17 oz.) can whole kernel corn
1 (14 oz.) can lima beans
1 medium potato, peeled and cut into small pieces
1 large onion, chopped
1/4 pound lean salt pork, cut into small pieces
Dash of cayenne pepper
1/2 cup water
2 tablespoons flour

- **Boil pork chops and chicken in four cups water in a Dutch oven until tender, about one hour.**
- Remove pork and chicken from the bones and discard the fat.
- **Add meat back to the liquid.**
- Add the undrained tomatoes, corn, and beans.
- **Add potato, onion, salt pork, salt and pepper and cayenne pepper.**
- Heat to boiling; reduce heat and simmer uncovered one hour.
- **Blend the flour and 1/2 cup water. (I like to shake it in a covered jar to mix well.)**
- Stir into the stew.
- **Bring back to a boil, stirring constantly for 1-2 minutes.**
- Serve hot.

MY GRANDSON, LIL' ART, LOVES THIS STEW.
IT'S A GREAT HEARTY RECIPE.

Old-Fashioned Vegetable Soup

1 pound stew meat or ground sirloin
1 large onion
2 stalks celery, chopped
2 (16 oz.) cans diced tomatoes
1 small package frozen butter beans
1 can green beans
4 large carrots, peeled and chopped
2 large potatoes, peeled and diced
1 small package frozen cut okra
4 medium yellow squash, coarsely chopped
1 can whole kernel corn, drained
1/2 cup cream corn
2 cans beef broth

- **Brown the meat.**

- If using stew meat, cook until tender, approximately one hour.

- **Add onion and let brown.**

- Add remaining ingredients and simmer in an open soup pot for about 45 minutes to one hour.

- **Add enough water to cover all ingredients and to make a good broth.**

You can substitute the full amount of cream corn for the whole kernel corn if you prefer.
Add it the last 15 minutes of cooking.
The yellow squash is what makes this vegetable soup stand out among others.
IT REALLY ADDS TO THE FLAVOR AND COLOR.

Dried Lima Beans & Rice Soup

1 pound bag dried lima beans
6-8 cups hot water
1 ham hock (or 2 slices country ham)
1 cup rice, uncooked
Salt to taste

- **Rinse and drain beans.**
- In a large pot, combine beans, water and ham. Soak overnight or at least 4 1/2 hours.
- **Simmer until beans are tender, approximately 1 1/2 to 2 hours.**
- Add salt sparingly because the ham will add some salt.
- **About 30 minutes before the beans are done, add the rice, stirring gently and occasionally.**
- The stirring will also help make the beans creamy.
- **You can keep adding hot water to make your soup as soupy as you like it.**

Soup Party

- **The hostess plans the date and time and boils the ham and beans.**
- Each guest is asked to bring one of the extras: bowls, hot cornbread, or a vegetable.
- **This is very little work for anyone, but everyone gets to enjoy!!!**

THIS DISH BECOMES A COMPLETE SOUTHERN MEAL
IF YOU ADD EXTRA HAM.

Strawberry Jello Salad

4 small boxes strawberry Jello
1 cup water
1 large can crushed pineapple, undrained
1 package frozen strawberries, thawed
4 bananas, mashed
2 cups sour cream

- **Bring water to a boil; dissolve Jello.**
- Add pineapple, strawberries, and fold in bananas.
- **Pour 1/2 of mixture in a 9 x 13 serving dish and refrigerate until Jello sets.**
- Spread sour cream on top of Jello, then pour remaining mixture of Jello over the sour cream.
- **Refrigerate until fully jelled.**

STRAWBERRY JELLO
SALAD

This is my FAMILY'S FAVORITE congealed salad.
It is served at almost every special get-together that we have.
It is served in a crystal cut glass bowl and it just adds
A BEAUTIFUL TOUCH TO OUR SERVING TABLE.

Raspberry Jello Salad

2 (3 oz.) packages raspberry gelatin
1 cup boiling water
1 (16 oz.) can whole cranberry sauce
1 small can crushed pineapple
1 cup pecans, chopped and roasted

- **Place gelatin in a bowl.**
- Add hot water and stir until completely dissolved.
- **Add the cranberry sauce and pineapple.**
- Fold in pecans.
- **Pour into a serving dish and refrigerate until well set.**

Broccoli Salad

2 bunches broccoli florets, washed very well
1 small bunch green onions, chopped
1 cup celery, chopped
1 1/2 cups grapes, halved (or 1 cup raisins)
6 slices bacon, fried and crumbled
1 cup mayonnaise
1/3 cup sugar
1 tablespoon vinegar
1 cup toasted almonds

- **Mix broccoli, green onions, celery, grapes or raisins, bacon, and 3/4 cup of the almonds in a bowl.**
- Mix mayonnaise, sugar and vinegar.
- **Pour over the salad and gently toss.**
- Sprinkle remaining 1/4 cup almonds on top.

Baby Spinach Salad

1 small bag fresh spinach
1 cup fresh strawberries
1 medium purple onion, sliced in rings
1 cup walnuts or slivered almonds, toasted

- **Wash the spinach and drain or spin really well.**
- Slice strawberries lengthwise, to retain shape.
- **Mix spinach, strawberries, onions, and nuts.**
- Add dressing.

DRESSING

3 tablespoons olive oil
1 tablespoon raspberry flavored vinegar
1 tablespoon lemon juice
3 tablespoons brown sugar

- **Combine all ingredients in a jar and shake to blend.**
- Refrigerate.
- **When ready to serve, pour dressing over salad.**
- Gently toss.

Country Layered Salad

1 head romaine lettuce, chopped
1 iceberg lettuce, chopped
5 boiled eggs, sliced or chopped
1 cup Swiss cheese, shredded
1 small bag frozen green peas, thawed and drained
1 small red onion, finely chopped
1 pound bacon, cooked and crumbled
1 cup purple cabbage, finely chopped
3 cups ranch dressing
1 pint of fresh grape tomatoes (whole)

- **Layer items in order listed.**
- Chill well.

Hint- I like to use whole grape tomatoes because if I have any leftovers it will stay fresh and not wilt because of the juice from the tomatoes.

THIS IS A WONDERFUL SALAD
that can be made ahead.
Just be sure to seal the salad with the ranch dressing.
Also, there are many other options to layer in the salad:
black olives, chopped cucumbers, shredded carrots.
FOR A MORE HEARTY SALAD,
add four cups of cooked macaroni or one cup of chopped ham or chicken.

PURPLE SLAW

MiMi's Purple Slaw

1 head green cabbage, finely chopped
1/4 head purple cabbage, finely chopped
1/2 cup sugar, or to taste
1 cup mayonnaise
1 teaspoon dry mustard
Salt and pepper to taste

- **Finely chop green and purple cabbage.**
- Mix mayonnaise, sugar, mustard, salt, pepper, and cabbage together. Mix well.
- **Add more mayonnaise, if needed, for your consistency.**
- Chill before serving.

Corn Bread Salad

4 cups romaine lettuce, finely chopped
4 medium tomatoes, chopped
1 green bell pepper, chopped
1 small purple onion, chopped
1/2 cup chopped sweet pickles
1 1/2 cup mayonnaise
1/4 cup sweet pickle juice
1 (8 oz.) package cornbread mix
12 slices bacon, fried and crumbled

- **Mix and bake the cornbread according to directions on the package; crumble.**
- Combine the tomatoes, green pepper, onions, bacon, and pickles.
- **Mix the mayonnaise and pickle juice.**
- Layer the ingredients in the following order: chopped lettuce, crumbled cornbread, tomato mixture, then cover with the mayonnaise mixture.
- **Cover and chill for 1 hour or overnight.**

CORN BREAD

SALAD

Chopped Green Salad

2 heads romaine lettuce, chopped
2 handfuls fresh spinach
2 cans mandarin oranges, drained
1 avocado, chopped
1 tablespoon purple onion, finely chopped
1/2 cup toasted slivered almonds

- **Combine all ingredients and mix well.**
- When ready to serve, toss with dressing.

DRESSING

3 tablespoons olive oil
1 tablespoon raspberry flavored vinegar
1 tablespoon lemon juice
3 teaspoons light brown sugar

- **Combine all ingredients in a jar and shake to blend.**
- Chill well before adding to the salad.

Romaine & Broccoli Salad WITH CRUNCHY NOODLES

1 package fresh broccoli, chopped
1 head romaine lettuce, chopped
Several green onions, chopped
1/2 cup extra virgin olive oil
1/4 cup honey
1/3 cup white wine vinegar
Salt and pepper to taste
1 (3 oz.) Ramen noodle soup mix (discard flavor packet)
1/4 cup butter
1 cup walnuts, coarsely broken

- **Mix lettuce, onion and broccoli.**
- Whisk together oil, honey, vinegar, salt and pepper.
- **Melt butter in a pan in a 350° oven.**
- Add broken noodles and walnuts.
- **Bake about 10 minutes, stirring occasionally, until lightly browned.**
- Let cool.
- **In a bowl, combine the lettuce mixture and the dressing and fold in the noodle and walnuts.**

BROCCOLI

Mixed Vegetable Salad

1 pound can cut green beans, drained
1 pound can cut wax beans, drained
1 (15 oz.) can kidney beans, drained
1 cup baby lima beans, cooked and drained
1 cup canned whole kernel corn, drained
1 cup carrots, sliced
3 medium purple onions, chopped
3 medium green peppers, chopped
1 cup vinegar
1 cup sugar
1/2 cup vegetable oil or extra virgin olive oil

- **Combine vegetables in a large bowl and toss lightly.**
- Combine vinegar, sugar and oil in a small saucepan and bring to a boil.
- **Pour hot marinade over vegetables and mix lightly.**
- Cover and chill overnight.

ART LOVES THIS SALAD. THIS IS HIS FAVORITE.
YOU CAN ALSO ADD THIS MIXTURE OVER YOUR CHOPPED SALAD
FOR A DIFFERENT TWIST.

Honey Mustard Dressing

1/2 cup mayonnaise
2 teaspoons Dijon mustard
2 tablespoons honey

- **Combine all ingredients and beat until smooth.**
- Chill until ready to serve.

SERVE OVER YOUR FAVORITE
TOSSED GREEN SALAD LETTUCE, TOMATO, ONIONS,
CUCUMBERS, AND A LITTLE SHREDDED CHEESE
AND OF COURSE FINELY CHOPPED PURPLE CABBAGE

ALWAYS GOOD.

YOU CAN ALSO PURCHASE A CONTAINER
OF THIS DRESSING AT THE RESTAURANT.

CAESAR SALAD

Waica's Caesar Salad Dressing

1 cup mayonnaise
2 tablespoons lemon juice
Salt and pepper to taste
1 teaspoon worcestershire sauce
1/2 teaspoon garlic, minced
1/2 cup parmesan cheese
1/2 cup extra virgin olive oil

- **Mix all ingredients and chill.**
- Toss your fresh, chopped and spun romaine lettuce with dressing.
- **Top with fresh grated parmesan and homemade croutons.**

Homemade Croutons

- **Using any sliced bread you have at home, cut into 1-inch by 1-inch squares.**
- Place one layer on a sheet pan. Brush with a small amount of butter. Sprinkle some garlic salt and paprika over the bread, and toast in the oven until golden brown.

Creamy Bleu Cheese

Yield: 3 cups

1/2 cup sour cream
1/2 cup mayonnaise
1/2 cup buttermilk
1/2 tablespoon vinegar (white wine vinegar)
1 teaspoon lemon juice
1 dash hot sauce
2 tablespoons sugar
1/2 wedge bleu cheese, crumbled

- **Mix all ingredients, except the bleu cheese, and blend well.**
- Fold in the cheese and refrigerate until well chilled.

Most of my family prefers bleu cheese dressing on their salad,
and when Waica came up with this one,

WE ALL JUST FELL IN LOVE WITH IT.

It's great served over a lettuce wedge topped with diced
tomatoes and crumbled "real" bacon, not bacon bits.

MiMi's CANNED CREAM SALAD DRESSING

1/2 cup canned cream (evaporated milk)
2 tablespoons sugar
2 teaspoons red wine vinegar

- Mix all ingredients together and chill.

Hint:
You can use light brown sugar instead of regular sugar,
and the red wine vinegar will give the dressing a pretty pale pink color.

SIMPLE-VERY FRENCH, AND DELICIOUS.

MiMi's THOUSAND ISLAND DRESSING

1 cup mayonnaise
1/2 cup catsup
1 tablespoon purple onion, finely chopped (optional)
2 tablespoons green olives, finely chopped (optional)
4 – 6 hard boiled eggs, chopped- yes lots of eggs
1/4 cup sweet pickled relish, finely chopped

- **Mix all ingredients and chill.**

I always use lots of chopped boiled eggs, but you can use two if you prefer.
My dressing is almost like an egg salad, which is just the way my family likes it.
But most of all, my Michael and Art love it. They say to their MiMi,

"THAT'S MIGHTY FINE."

Cucumber Dressing

1/2 cup mayonnaise
1/2 cup sour cream
1 cup cucumber, finely minced
1 tablespoon fresh lemon juice
1 tablespoon sugar

- **Mix all ingredients and chill.**
- You may also add 1/2 teaspoon dill or 1/2 teaspoon chives to change the taste just a little.

THIS IS A SPECIAL DRESSING TO SERVE OVER ICEBERG LETTUCE WEDGES.
SPRINKLE DRESSED LETTUCE LIGHTLY WITH PAPRIKA BEFORE SERVING.

Raspberry Vinaigrette

1 part Southern Raspberry Mix
2 parts white vinegar
1/2 cup vegetable oil or extra virgin olive oil

- **Mix all ingredients and chill.**

- Toss with your favorite salad greens.

- **This is also good on fresh spinach salad, and you can add canned mandarin oranges or fresh strawberries.**

- Top with chopped dates or toasted almonds for a finishing touch.

- **Optional fresh raspberries for garnish on salad.**

The Southern Raspberry Mix is what we use to make
OUR FAMOUS RASPBERRY TEA.

You can purchase it at The Ivy House Restaurant, and it comes with a recipe guide full of unique ways to use this mix.

MiMi's Salad Dressing

1 cup mayonnaise
1/3 cup balsamic vinegar
1/2 cup water
1/4 cup sugar
1/3 cup parmesan cheese
2 tablespoons salad oil or extra virgin olive oil
Salt and pepper to taste

- **Mix all ingredients in a jar and shake well.**
- Chill.
- **When ready to serve, just pour the dressing on the salad of your choice and mix lightly.**

A Special Cranberry Dressing

3/4 cup salad oil or extra virgin olive oil
1/4 cup wine vinegar
1 cup canned whole cranberries
1/2 teaspoon salt
1/2 teaspoon paprika
1 teaspoon sugar

- **Blend all ingredients together in a blender or shake in a jar.**
  (I prefer to use a jar so the berries stay whole.)
- **Chill.**

A quick version of this old recipe is to mix one bottle of Italian dressing with one pound of whole cranberries.
SHAKE IN A JAR AND CHILL.

83

Vegetables, Starches & Pastas

Scalloped Tomatoes

1 large can diced tomatoes
1/2 tube Saltines, crushed
1/2 stick butter
1/2 cup sugar
Salt and pepper to taste

- **Mix ingredients in a sauce pan and bring to a gentle boil.**
- Continue to cook until liquid is absorbed and mixture has thickened.

Tomato Gravy

1 (14.5 oz.) can diced tomatoes
6 oz. canned cream (evaporated milk)
2 tablespoons flour
1 cup water
1 stick butter
Salt and pepper to taste

- **In a sauce pan, mix all ingredients and cook over medium heat until smooth and bubbly.**

Delicious served with fried pork chops or country fried cubed steak.
You can add the can of tomatoes and cream, along with the flour, directly to the frying pan.
After cooking your chops or steaks, just pour off almost all the frying grease, leaving the crusty particles.
Stir all ingredients until smooth. Cook on medium heat until thickened.
Add water, until right consistency.

Company Peas

2 cans tiny English peas
1 (3 oz.) package cream cheese
1/2 stick butter
Salt and pepper to taste

- **Melt the cream cheese and butter in a sauce pan.**
- Drain peas and add to mixture.
- **Add salt and pepper and heat thoroughly.**

COMPANY PEAS

TO MAKE A REALLY SPECIAL DISH,
you can bake pastry puff shells. Spoon peas into shells and place on the plate.

To make the shells, simply roll out a pastry crust, cut off small pieces and lightly butter one side,
pressing the crust into a sprayed muffin tin and baking at 350° until lightly browned.

ADD A LITTLE CHOPPED PIMENTO FOR COLOR.

Nutty Stuffed Mushrooms

1 pound large, fresh mushrooms
2 tablespoons extra virgin olive oil
3 cloves garlic, minced
1/2 cup chopped nuts
3 tablespoons butter
1 cup Pepperidge Farm Herb Seasoning Stuffing
3/4 cup shredded Italian-blend cheese
1 large egg, beaten
Salt and pepper to taste

- **Rinse mushrooms and place on paper towel to drain.**

- Remove stems and set aside.

- **Sprinkle inside of mushroom with salt and then brush them with olive oil.**

- Chop stems, saute with garlic and nuts in butter over medium heat for 3-4 minutes.

- **Remove from heat and add stuffing, cheese and egg.**

- Mix well and spoon into mushrooms.

- **Bake on ungreased baking sheet at 350° 8-10 minutes.**

- Serve immediately.

We serve these frequently at home and at the Ivy House for special occasions.
They are wonderful to have at rehearsal dinners, birthday suppers,
and any other time that you are serving your favorite steak or prime rib.

We made these for Joe Joe Knauff for a dinner party at home.
GLEN HARRIS STILL REMEMBERS HOW GOOD THEY WERE.
He was one of the groomsmen for the wedding.

Sweet Potato Fritters

2 1/2 cups self-rising flour
1 cup self-rising cornmeal
2 tablespoons sugar
3/4 teaspoon ground ginger
1/4 teaspoon ground cinnamon
1/4 teaspoon ground nutmeg
2 1/4 cups sweet potatoes, cooked, peeled and cubed
2 cups buttermilk
3 large eggs
Peanut oil for frying

- **Combine first six ingredients in a large bowl.**
- Stir in sweet potatoes.
- **Whisk together the buttermilk and eggs.**
- Add to flour mixture, stirring just until moistened.
- **Pour oil to a depth of one inch into a deep cast-iron skillet.**
- Heat to 350° and drop dough by rounded tablespoonfuls into hot oil.
- **Fry 1 1/2 minutes on each side or until golden brown.**
- Drain well on paper towels .
- **Keep fritters warm but not soggy on the bottom by placing on a wire rack over a baking sheet and placing in a 200° oven.**

Baked Tiny Crook Neck Squash

12 – 15 crook neck yellow squash, sliced in half lengthwise
1 (12 oz.) canned cream (evaporated milk)
Salt and pepper to taste

- **Place squash halves in a single layer in a shallow baking dish.**
- Cover with milk, salt and pepper.
- **Bake uncovered 25-30 minutes at 350°.**
- Use crook neck squash only. No substitutions.

Green String Bean Bundles

2 (16 oz.) cans whole green beans, drained
(or whole fresh green beans, slightly cooked)
6 slices bacon, cut in half and slightly cooked
1 cup brown sugar
Salt and pepper to taste

- **Arrange beans in twelve bundles in a baking pan.**
- Wrap each bundle with a bacon slice and secure with toothpick.
- **Sprinkle brown sugar on each bundle.**
- Bake at 400° until bacon has finished cooking.

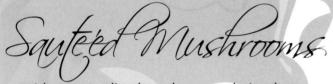

Sautéed Mushrooms

1 large can sliced mushrooms, drained
1 large onion, diced
1 tablespoon butter
1 tablespoon extra virgin olive oil
1 tablespoon sugar
1 tablespoon worcestershire sauce

- **Saute onion in butter, olive oil and sugar until tender.**
- Add mushrooms, stirring well.
- **Allow to stir fry for a few minutes.**
- Add the worcestershire sauce and simmer about 15 minutes more.

DELICIOUS SERVED OVER A GRILLED
HAMBURGER STEAK OR ANY OTHER STEAK.

Baked Sweet Onion Custard

3 ounces shredded cheese (parmesan or cheddar)
2 cups canned cream (evaporated milk) or whipping
cream
6 large eggs
1/3 cup plain flour
2 tablespoons sugar
2 teaspoons baking powder
1 teaspoon salt (or to taste)
1/4 cup butter
1/4 cup extra virgin olive oil
6 medium sweet onions, chopped fine

- **Mix together the cheese, cream and eggs.**
- Mix flour, sugar, baking powder and salt and add to the cheese mixture.
- **In a large frying pan, cook onions in butter and olive oil until lightly browned, stirring frequently.**
- Add onions to mixture and pour into a sprayed 9 x 13 baking dish.
- **Bake at 350° for 25-30 minutes.**

THIS IS *Evelyn's* FAVORITE!

Squash Dressing

2 cups yellow squash, sliced
1 medium onion, chopped
1/2 cup water
2 cups cornbread crumbs or stuffing mix
1 can cream of chicken soup
1/2 cup butter, melted
1 cup shredded cheddar cheese, optional

- **Saute onion in butter on medium heat until tender; add squash and water and simmer until tender; drain and mash out any excess water.**

- Add the cornbread crumbs, soup, salt and pepper.

- **Pour into a 9 x 13 baking dish and bake at 325° for 25 minutes.**

- Sprinkle with cheese the last 10 minutes of baking.

Fried Green Tomato Bake

Yield: 4-6 servings

1 cup flour
1 egg
1 cup milk
2 teaspoons sugar
Salt and pepper to taste
4 firm green tomatoes, cut into 3/4" slices
1/4 cup vegetable oil or bacon fat (it's the best)
1/4 cup olive oil
1 cup canned cream (evaporated milk)
Parsley for garnish

- **Mix flour, sugar, salt and pepper.**
- Mix egg and milk.
- **Dip the tomatoes in the egg mixture then in the flour mixture.**
- Heat the vegetable oil (or bacon fat), and the olive oil in a 10" skillet until hot.
- **Fry the tomatoes until golden brown.**
- Remove from the skillet and place in a shallow baking dish and keep warm.
- **Heat canned cream to boiling in the same skillet used to fry the tomatoes.**
- Pour over tomatoes, and bake for 20 minutes at **350°**.
  Sprinkle of parsley and serve.

BRITTANY, MY GRANDDAUGHTER, IS MY EGGPLANT GIRL.
SHE LOVES ANYTHING THAT HAS TO DO WITH EGGPLANT.

Eggplant Casserole

2 large eggplants, sliced into 1/2 slices
2 cups spaghetti sauce
3 medium onions, sliced
1 cup shredded mozzarella cheese
1/2 cup grated parmesan cheese
Salt and pepper to taste

- **Boil eggplant slices for 10 minutes; drain. Layer in 9 x 13 baking dish half of the eggplant, onion, sauce, and mozzarella cheese.**
- Repeat layers.
- **Top with parmesan cheese.**
- Bake in a preheated oven at 350° for 45 minutes.
- **This recipe is truly a hit. My granddaughter, Brittany, just loves it.**

Lima Beans & Ham Hocks

2 pounds smoked ham hocks
6 cups water
1 pound dried lima beans (soak over night)
1 large onion, chopped
1 1/2 teaspoons dry mustard
1 clove garlic, finely chopped
Salt and pepper to taste

- **Heat the ham hocks and water to boiling in a 4-quart pot, reduce heat, cover and simmer 30 minutes.**
- Add beans and heat to boiling. Add onion, mustard, garlic, salt and pepper.
- **Cover and simmer until beans are tender, 1 to 2 hours, depending on the age of dried beans.**
- Keep beans covered with water while simmering, stirring occasionally.
- **Remove the hocks, trim pork from bones, and return the meat back to the beans**
- Water in beans vary according to your liking. More water for extra soupy beans or less water for thicker soup beans.

My family likes to have our beans over rice for supper and topped off with chopped onions, but when Waica married Zack, he brought his family tradition to ours by adding a dollop of mayonnaise on top of the beans, rice and onions, and,

OH, MY GOSH, IT IS SO GOOD MIXING IT ALL UP TOGETHER.

IT GIVES YOU THIS CREAMY EFFECT THAT IS JUST MOUTH-WATERING.
ADD A DROP OF YOUR FAVORITE PEPPER SAUCE TO HEAT UP A LITTLE- YUM!

THIS VEGETABLE GOES WELL WITH A NICE RICE DISH,

LIKE OUR SAVORY RICE.

Summertime Vegetables

2 cups sliced yellow squash
2 cups sliced zucchini
1 cup fresh tomato, chopped
1 clove garlic, minced
1/2 cup green pepper, julienne sliced
1/4 stick butter
1 tablespoon olive oil
1 tablespoon fresh basil, or 1 teaspoon dried

- **Spray a large skillet (I like to use our old black iron skillet) and heat until hot.**
- Add butter, olive oil and garlic.
- **Cook 1 minute.**
- Add squash, zucchini, tomatoes and green pepper.
- **Cook and stir until vegetables are crisp-tender.**
- Sprinkle with basil.

Old-Fashioned Mixed Greens

1 bunch fresh collard greens, chopped
1 head fresh cabbage, chopped
1 pound ham hocks
Salt and pepper to taste
1 quart water

- **Wash and cook greens at least 3-5 times, according to how clean they are.**
- Cook collard greens and ham in water, salt and pepper for at least 1 hour, or until tender. (Cooking time depends on the age of the greens when they were picked.)
- **Add a little more water, if needed, to keep greens covered while cooking.**
- This also makes a good pot liquor.
- **Add chopped cabbage and boil gently another 20 minutes.**
- Serve hot with buttermilk cornbread, baked golden brown in a black skillet with lots of butter spread on top.

My mama cooked fresh mustard greens the same way, but used sliced white bacon instead of ham hocks.

After they were done, instead of adding cabbage, she mixed some of the pot liquor with plain meal and dropped it by the spoonfuls into the gently boiling greens to make dumplings.

DELICIOUS, SOUTHERN STYLE.

THIS DISH IS **ESPECIALLY DELICIOUS** WITH HAM. FOR CONVENIENCE, THE CASSEROLE CAN BE ASSEMBLED AND REFRIGERATED OVERNIGHT BEFORE BAKING.

Southern Scalloped Pineapple

Yield: 8 servings

5 cups fresh bread crumbs, no crust
1 (20 oz.) can pineapple tidbits
4 eggs, beaten
1 1/2 cups sugar
1/2 cup canned cream (evaporated milk)
1 cup butter, melted

- **Toss together bread crumbs and pineapple and place in a casserole baking dish.**
- Combine eggs, sugar, butter and pour over the pineapple mixture.
- **Bake uncovered at 350° for 30 minutes.**

Cream Style Corn

Yield: 6 servings

2 (10 oz.) packages frozen whole kernel corn creamed in a food processor
3/4 cup canned cream (evaporated milk) or whipping cream
1 1/2 teaspoon sugar
1 teaspoon salt
1 1/2 teaspoon corn starch

- **Cook corn partially done according to package directions.**
- Combine cream, sugar and salt and corn starch and blend.
- **Add slowly to corn until thickened and bubbly, about 2 minutes•**
- Cook and stir until thickened and bubbly, about 2 minutes.
- **Taste like fresh creamed corn off the cob!**

CREAM STYLE CORN

THIS IS MY EVELYN'S FAVORITE SIDE DISH.
NO MATTER WHAT OCCASION IT IS, SHE WANTS CREAM CORN.
SHE RELISHED IT EVEN WHEN SHE WAS A LITTLE GIRL.

Stir-Fry Ribbon Vegetables

3 large yellow squash, sliced deeply with a potato peeler
3 large zucchini, sliced deeply with a potato peeler
3 large carrots, peeled and sliced deeply with a potato peeler
1/2 stick butter
2 tablespoons olive oil
1 teaspoon rosemary, thyme and chopped parsley

- **Heat butter and olive oil in skillet.**
- Add vegetables and cook until tender, stirring gently.
- **Add herbs before serving. (Thinly-sliced onions are also good added to this dish.)**

Tomato Pie

Yield: 4 servings

1 9-inch dish frozen pie shell
3 medium ripe tomatoes, sliced
6 strips bacon, fried and crumbled
1 cup grated sharp cheddar cheese
1 cup mayonnaise

- **Bake frozen pie shell following package directions.**
- Place tomatoes in bottom of pie shell: top with crumbled bacon.
- **Combine cheese and mayonnaise and pour over tomatoes.**
- Bake 35-40 minutes in a preheated 350º oven.

The Ivy House Savory Rice

2 cups Uncle Ben's Rice
1/2 cup mayonnaise
1/2 cup sour cream
1/2 jar pimentos, chopped
2 tablespoons chives

- **Cook rice according to package directions.**
- Mix last 4 ingredients and add to the hot rice, blending well.

This rice is delicious because of the consistency of the rice.
You can pack this rice in any shape mold that you have.

THIS MAKES A BEAUTIFUL PLATE PRESENTATION
and also great for children's plates for funny shapes.

We serve this rice at the restaurant.
Many of our shrimp scampi customers rave over the flavor,
AND I BET YOU WILL TOO!

Onion & Rice Casserole

1 cup rice, uncooked
2 cups water
7 medium size sweet onions, sliced
1 stick butter
2 tablespoons olive oil
4 ounces swiss cheese, grated
2 cups canned cream (evaporated milk)
Salt to taste

- **Saute onions in butter and olive oil until translucent.**
- Combine the rice and water, onions, salt, cheese and cream.
- **Spread in a buttered 9 x 13 baking dish and bake at 325° for 1 hour.**

Oven Fried Okra

1 large package frozen cut okra
1/4 cup vegetable oil or bacon grease
Salt and pepper to taste

- **Place the okra in a sprayed ovenproof pan. Add the vegetable oil, olive oil, salt and pepper.**
- Baked in a preheated 400° oven until okra is tender.
- **Stir occasionally.**

Double Squash CASSEROLE WITH ALMONDS

Yield: 4-6 servings

1 pound green zuchinni squash, sliced
1 pound yellow squash, sliced
1/4 cup butter
1/2 cup canned cream (evaporated milk)
1 small onion, chopped
Salt and pepper to taste
2 eggs, beaten
2 cups grated cheddar cheese
4 ounces slivered almonds
10 buttery round crackers, crushed
1 tablespoon butter, melted

- **Boil squash for 10 minutes or until tender; drain. Add butter, milk, onion, salt and pepper to squash.**
- Blend in eggs.
- **Add cheese.**
- Spoon mixture into 9 x 13 casserole dish.
- **Bake at 350° for 20 minutes.**
- Toss crackers in butter and sprinkle on top.
- **Sprinkle almonds on top.**
- Bake at 350° for 10 additional minutes.

Baked Tomato Slices

Yield: 6 servings

6 slices tomatoes, 1" thick
6 thin slices sweet onion
6 heaping teaspoons brown sugar
6 drops worchestershire sauce
6 dashes Italian seasoning
6 scoops bread crumbs
6 tablespoons grated parmesan cheese
Salt and pepper to taste

- **Arrange tomato slices in a shallow baking pan, well greased with olive oil.**
- Stack layers as listed above.
- **Bake at 350° for 30 minutes.**

Baked Acorn Squash

Yield: 4 servings

2 acorn squash
4 tablespoons maple syrup
4 tablespoons canned cream (evaporated milk)

- **Heat oven to 350°.**
- Cut each squash in half, remove seeds and fibers.
- **Place squash cut sides up in an ungreased pan.**
- Spoon 1 tablespoon syrup and 1 tablespoon cream into each half.
- **Bake uncovered until tender, about 1 hour.**

Hot Fruit Compote

Yield: 15 servings

1 (16-oz.) package dried pitted prunes
1 (16-oz.) package dried apricots
1 (13-oz.) can pineapple chunks, undrained
1 (8-oz.) can mandarin oranges, undrained
1 (16-oz.) can cherry pie filling
1 cup grape juice
1/3 cup nuts, optional

- **Chop prunes and apricots into bite-size pieces.**
- Mix all ingredients in a large bowl and pour into a 9 x 13 casserole dish.
- **Bake at 300° for 45 minutes.**

At the Ivy House we use this recipe on a lot of our catering jobs.
Adds a special touch to the menu, goes great with our ham and pork.
We like serving it during the fall and winter months.

Quick Crispy Cabbage

1 medium green cabbage, shredded
1 tablespoon butter or bacon grease
Salt and pepper to taste

- **Cook cabbage with butter or bacon grease in a 10" skillet over medium heat, stirring often.**

- Cover and simmer, stirring occasionally, until cabbage is crisp-tender, about 10 minutes.

- **Salt and pepper. If you desire, add a little canned cream. Oh, so good!**

- To turn this dish into a baked cabbage casserole, just saute 1 large, chopped onion in 2 tablespoons butter and 2 tablespoons light olive oil.

- **Add 1/3 cup flour and 1 cup canned cream (evaporated milk).**

- Add to the cabbage and pour into a 9 x 13 inch baking dish and bake 30 minutes at 350°.

- **Top with shredded cheddar cheese. Bake until melted.**

An Ivy House Favorite

MiMi's Creamy Macaroni & Cheese

Yield: 12 servings

1 (16-oz.) box macaroni
1 egg, beaten
3-4 cups milk
8 ounces Velveeta cheese, cubed
2 cups shredded cheddar cheese
1 stick butter (Yes, I'm Sorry!)
1 teaspoon flour

- **Boil noodles as directed on package; rinse and drain. Cook a little al dente.**
- Pour into a 9 x 13 sprayed baking dish.
- **Mix eggs, flour and milk together; add the cheeses and pour over noodles.**
- The milk should almost cover noodles. Add a little more, if necessary.
- **Cut butter into small pieces and dot the top. Bake 45 minutes at 325°.**

Evelyn and Waica

USUALLY MAKE THESE FOR OUR FAMILY
GET-TOGETHERS AND BIRTHDAYS.
WHEN THE MEN GRILL THE STEAKS,
WE HAVE THESE. THEY GO GREAT TOGETHER.

Creamy Stuffed Potatoes

Yield: 6 servings

6 medium baking potatoes
1 (3-oz.) package cream cheese
1 stick butter
1 cup sour cream
1 cup shredded cheddar cheese
Canned cream (evaporated milk)

- **Bake the potatoes until tender.**
- Cut the top off of the potato and scoop out pulp and place in a bowl, reserving shells.
- **Mix pulp, cream cheese, butter, sour cream, salt and pepper until well blended.**
- Add canned cream to get them to a creamy consistency.
- **Spoon pulp mixture back into the shells. Bake at 300° for 10-15 minutes or until thoroughly heated.**
- Top them with shredded cheese and bake until melted.

Ann's Scalloped Potatoes

6 cups thinly sliced potatoes
Milk
Garlic salt and black pepper
1/3 cup butter
1/3 cup flour

- **In a 9 x 13 baking dish, place sliced potatoes.**
- Sprinkle with garlic salt, black pepper, and flour on top of potatoes.
- **Pour enough milk to cover potatoes, with butter on top.**
- Bake at 350° for 40-45 minutes.

SCALLOPED POTATOES

I stir potatoes slightly, after they begin to get tender,
and then sprinkle some shredded cheese if you would like.

THE GARLIC SALT IS REALLY WHAT MAKES THIS RECIPE DELICIOUS.
I would also add more butter, of course.

Candied Sweet Potatoes

6 medium sweet potatoes
1 1/2 cup packed brown sugar
3 tablespoons butter
3 tablespoons water
1/2 teaspoon salt
Apple pie spice

- **Wash your sweet potatoes good, then rub them with vegetable oil and place them on a sheet pan and bake on 350⁰ until tender.**

- Peel or pull off skins and cut potatoes into 1/2 inch slices and place in a 9x13.

- **Heat sugar, butter, water and salt in a small skillet over medium heat, stirring constantly until smooth and bubbly.**

- Pour mixture over potatoes and sprinkle with apple pie spice and bake at 300⁰ for 20-25 minutes.

15-MINUTE
Creamy Fettuccini Alfredo

1 (8-oz.) package fettuccini pasta
1/2 cup butter
3/4 cup grated parmesan cheese
1/2 cup half & half or evaporated milk (canned cream)
1 (8-oz.) package cream cheese, cubed
Salt and pepper to taste

- **Combine butter, cheeses, half & half, salt and pepper in sauce pan over medium heat, stirring well to blend.**
- Cook until hot, but not boiling.
- **Cook pasta according to package directions.**
- Rinse and combine with the cream sauce. Serve hot.

A LOT OF MY FAMILY MEMBERS ARE FETTUCCINI NUTS,
but not like my Micala. She truly loves this recipe and she could eat it several times a week.

WE EVEN HAD TO BRING HER FETTUCCINI TO THE HOSPITAL
when she had our sweet little blonde-headed, blue-eyed boy, Grayson.

And she has recently given me another great grandson,
RADLEE, SUCH A SWEET BABY!

VEGETABLES, STARCHES & PASTAS

...Family ...Life ...History

My life...

...began on November 26, 1933. I was delivered by Dr. Willis, just three miles southeast of Williston, on the edge of Marion County. This was a time when doctors still came to your house to deliver babies. I had one brother, Lawton, whom I worshiped, and two sisters, Dott and Nettie. I was the baby. There are over 13 years between me and my brother and sisters. They were half-grown by the time I came along, so I was alot like an only child growing up. But we were all very close.

Nettie, Lawton, Dott/N, & Margorie Kay

My family moved down the road to Emathla when I was a young child. The city bus would pick me up on the Emathla corner and I would ride it all the way to downtown Ocala. When the bus dropped me off, I would go down the street to get my breakfast. Mama would give me 15 cents every morning so I could buy a doughnut and a glass of milk at Bitting's Drug Store on my walk to school.

Retail became a part of my life at a very early age. My Daddy rented the grocery store there on the corner in Emathla, right beside our home. I always wanted to have a grocery store of my own one day. I loved stacking all the cans, making sure all of the labels were turned the right way. But even as a small child, I always said, "I will never sell beer or wine in my grocery store." Little did I know that you had to sell beer and wine to make it in the grocery store business. Needless to say, I have never owned one. I just never liked alcohol. It makes the sweetest people turn sour, and my Daddy didn't want Mama and me around it at all.

Customers would come into the store, after having a little bit too much to drink, and Daddy would look at Mama and me with those big brown eyes, and we knew we had to go to the back room. Daddy was very protective of mother and me.

In my teenage years, we moved to Dunnellon, where Daddy purchased a larger grocery store. I attended Dunnellon High School and loved to wear pretty clothes everyday. I still do! But pretty clothes cost money. So, when I was 15, I would catch the Greyhound bus to Williston on Fridays to stay with Nettie and work weekends in her restaurant, THE CHICK INN. The building is gone now, but it used to be located right on Noble Avenue in downtown Williston. There are gas pumps now sitting in that same spot.

DR. J.M. Willis

Freda Roach Studstill Hogan & DR. J.M. Willis 1940

Sprinkle
a
Spoonful
of
Love

Dedicated to my Precious Sister
Nettii Griffin

DEDICATED TO MY SISTER

Nettie Griffin

ORIGINAL OWNER OF
"CHICK INN" RESTAURANT
FOR 40 YEARS.

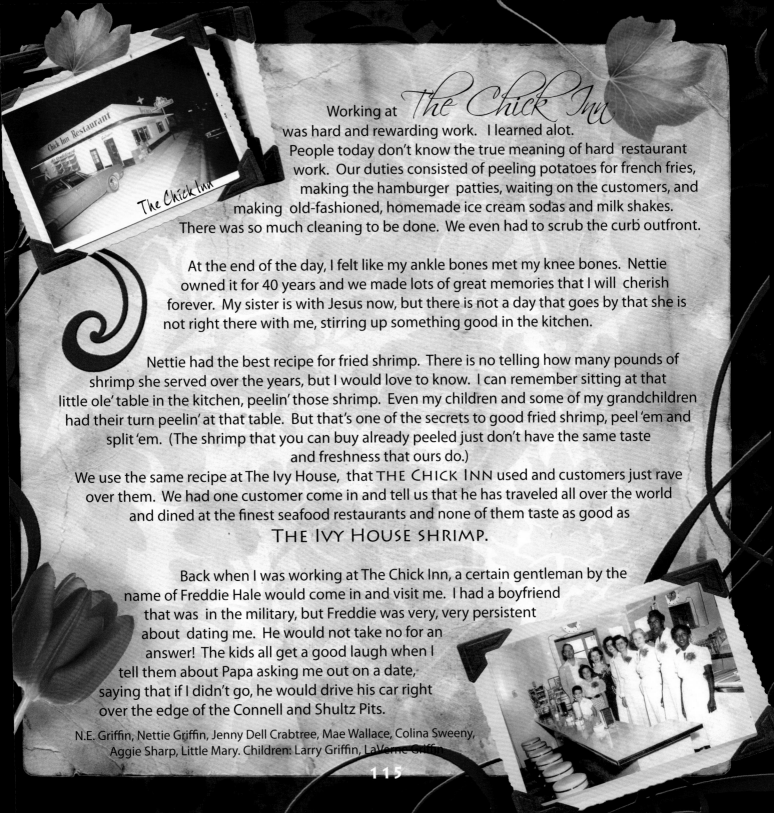

Working at *The Chick Inn* was hard and rewarding work. I learned alot.

People today don't know the true meaning of hard restaurant work. Our duties consisted of peeling potatoes for french fries, making the hamburger patties, waiting on the customers, and making old-fashioned, homemade ice cream sodas and milk shakes. There was so much cleaning to be done. We even had to scrub the curb outfront.

At the end of the day, I felt like my ankle bones met my knee bones. Nettie owned it for 40 years and we made lots of great memories that I will cherish forever. My sister is with Jesus now, but there is not a day that goes by that she is not right there with me, stirring up something good in the kitchen.

Nettie had the best recipe for fried shrimp. There is no telling how many pounds of shrimp she served over the years, but I would love to know. I can remember sitting at that little ole' table in the kitchen, peelin' those shrimp. Even my children and some of my grandchildren had their turn peelin' at that table. But that's one of the secrets to good fried shrimp, peel 'em and split 'em. (The shrimp that you can buy already peeled just don't have the same taste and freshness that ours do.)

We use the same recipe at The Ivy House, that THE CHICK INN used and customers just rave over them. We had one customer come in and tell us that he has traveled all over the world and dined at the finest seafood restaurants and none of them taste as good as

THE IVY HOUSE SHRIMP.

Back when I was working at The Chick Inn, a certain gentleman by the name of Freddie Hale would come in and visit me. I had a boyfriend that was in the military, but Freddie was very, very persistent about dating me. He would not take no for an answer! The kids all get a good laugh when I tell them about Papa asking me out on a date, saying that if I didn't go, he would drive his car right over the edge of the Connell and Shultz Pits.

N.E. Griffin, Nettie Griffin, Jenny Dell Crabtree, Mae Wallace, Colina Sweeny, Aggie Sharp, Little Mary. Children: Larry Griffin, LaVerne Griffin

The Chick Inn

He and I courted for a while and got married when I was 18 and still in high school. We lived on his old family farm, where we raised our three girls, Ann, Myra and Evelyn. I stayed home with my girls, was a substitute bus driver, and worked the farm with a few of the farmhands that lived there. We worked hard to get the farm cleaned up and fenced so we could get some cows. After cleaning the farm, we would go to the Whitehurst farm and pick up grass sprigs from Elliot. I still think about how kind that was for him to give us all of those sprigs to plant on our farm. We planted peanuts, watermelons, and vegetables. We harvested and shipped them all over the country.

Michael Sr., Waica and Michael's daddy, drove the semi-truck to deliver the produce all over the country. I remember when Waica was about two years old, big Michael decided to take Ann and Waica on a delivery to Michigan with him. Waica was a very active child and Michael said she bounced and jumped all over the sleeper in the semi but they had a great time.

I MARRIED THE GREATEST ENCOURAGER. HE THOUGHT I COULD DO ANYTHING. SO I TRIED. WHEN MY GIRLS GOT A LITTLE OLDER, I DECIDED TO GET BACK TO WHAT I LOVE — RETAIL.

Mrs Jeannette Barton

$\mathcal{I}$n 1970, I purchased Jeannette's Dress Shop. The store was half gift shop, half dress shop. Mrs. Jeannette kept the gift shop and I had the dress side. We had a wonderful time together. Mrs. Ruby Wise, Mary Holder, and Roselee Stell worked in the shop as well. What dear memories, which I hold close to my heart. Several years later, I decided to sell the dress shop and started M. Hale Sod Corporation from the house. But my true love was still retail. One day, my youngest daughter, Evelyn, and I discovered that we could buy off-price clothing wholesale. We were so excited. We found a little building in Williston on the side street next to Perkins State Bank. It was perfect for what we wanted. Marv-e-Less Fashions evolved from there and was a great success. We were able to buy clothes at low prices and sell them for less. The concept was great. Evelyn, Myra, and I sold clothes to the teenage girls and our prissy missies and the golden girls as well. Evelyn and I stayed there from about 1988 to 1993. And then one day, on the way to the post office, I passed the big house that I had only dreamed of purchasing. All it took was for me to mention it in front of Freddie. HE THOUGHT THAT IT WAS A GREAT IDEA. We started researching to find the current owner. Gaylon Warner actually was living in the home and renovating it at the same time. He was willing to let us rent the home with the option to buy. We did, and bought it a couple of years later. We have been there ever since.

SOME OF OUR ROOMS AT THE

The Ivy House

Lodge Room

Grape Room

Grape Room

Veranda

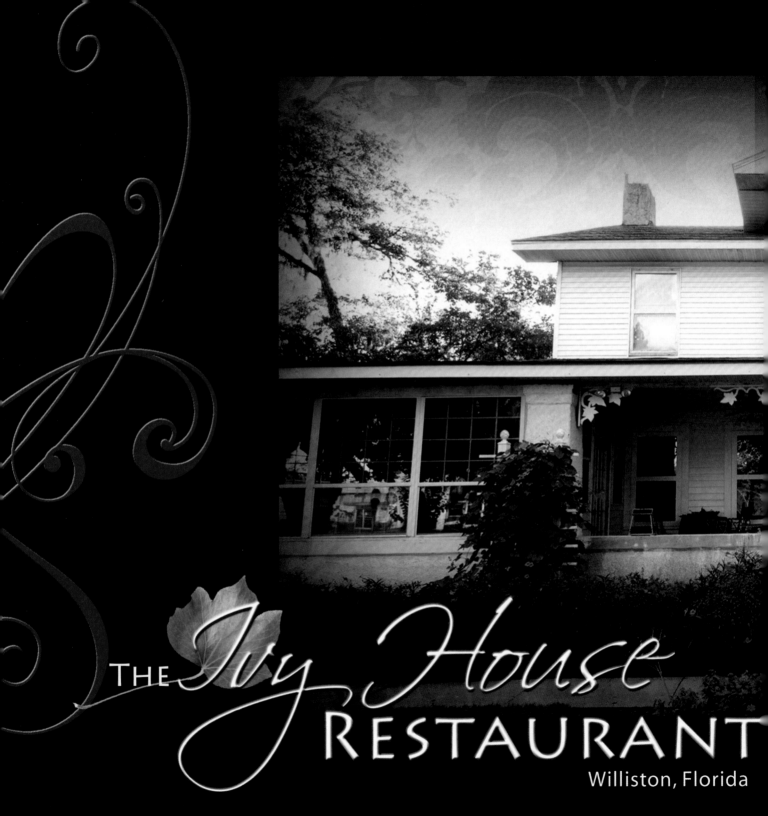

THE *Ivy House*
RESTAURANT

Williston, Florida

- The Ivy House was Established in 1993

- Built by Dr. James M. Willis in 1912

- Williston, Florida was founded and named in honor of Jesse M. Willis, father of Dr. Willis, in 1875

We started with two dining areas, The Grape Room and The Lodge Room, a boutique downstairs and a gift shop upstairs. The first day of business was incredible. The hot meal consisted of sirloin tips over homemade mashed potatoes, mixed greens, sweet potatoes, garden salad, corny cornbread and a yeast roll. The cold plate was our Chicken Taco Salad. The meals were beautiful. Our servers that day were Ann, my first born, (I have to say that, she doesn't allow me to say my oldest daughter) and the Smith girls, Pam and Ginger.

"WHAT WONDERFUL FUN MEMORIES WE MADE!"

At that time, we opened for lunch on Thursdays and Fridays. My precious friend, Louis Reeves, who now is with Jesus after a hard battle with cancer, helped me run the entire kitchen, which was about a 10x15 room. Not only was it our cooking and dishwashing area, but the servers worked in there also. I would arrive a 5 a.m. to prepare the desserts and then lunch for the day. Customers would ask what was on tomorrow's menu and I would reply "something good"! Back then we did not have delivery trucks for all our supplies so I would go to the store every afternoon to buy something special for the next day.

Shortly after opening, in the latter part of 1993, we extended our business hours and days to accomodate all of our customers. We began opening Tuesdays through Saturday for lunch and now we are serving weekend nights and lunch seven days a week. What started as a hobby became a full-fledged business.

"I LOVE EVERY MINUTE OF IT!"

Everyday continued to get busier and busier. My granddaughter, Waica, worked at the Levy County State Bank at the time and was attending Central Florida Community College. She would come to The Ivy House on her 30 minute lunch break and help me fix plates the whole time, never having time to actually eat. Finally, she came to me and said, "Mimi, I can go to college anytime. I think I need to come here and help you." She has been with me ever since, right by my side. We make a great team in the kitchen. I taught her everything and she can cook just as well as I can!

For the last fifteen years, we have had many employees that have helped us in the kitchen, but none like my Dora. She is a work force like no other. She and several of her family members manage our kitchen. They are like part of our family and we are very blessed to have them.

6 *My middle daughter,* Myra, came down from Tennessee to be a server and our dessert baker. Now she bakes full time and what a wonderful job she has done. Her desserts--WOW! They're amazing! My other girls, Evelyn and Ann, handle the front end of the house and all of the precious customers. Ann is a wonderful hostess. She greets everyone with that southern charm that people long for. Evelyn is also the buyer for the boutique. She loves pretty clothes, just like me, and has always had a passion for jewelry. Evelyn would go with me to work at Jeannette's Dress Shop when she was only four years old. Customers would try on outfits and ask, "Does this look good?" And she would say, "No, that doesn't match," or "That doesn't look good on you." Everyone knows she is a fanatic for color coordination.

Micala and Alesha, my other granddaughters, have waitressed, off and on, through the years. Micala has been a main server for several years now. She is a hard worker. Waica is over all catering jobs and Micala is is an important part of her team. My precious Brittany has worked as our bookkeeper and has also waitressed. After having her three little darling children, she had to leave us, but she promised her MiMi she would come back.

We are so blessed to have our family all working together. Life is so fast and busy these days. When work is over, we all have our individual families to take care of. But getting to spend quality time together at work is truly a blessing from God. The Ivy House staff have done such a great job helping build this business into something spectacular.

Our gift shop and boutique are now located upstairs and managed by my dear friends, Bettye Harris and Nell Cain. I call them my sisters. They are a great team, but watch out! Mrs. Bettye will sell the shirt off your back if you're not careful. Our downstairs is now strictly restaurant seating. We added The Rose Room, which used to be the boutique. The Rose Room is decorated with hand-painted rose vines on the walls. This unique room is used every day for lunch, but we also use it often for special bridal luncheons.

Evelyn, MiMi and Ann

Bettye Harris

Nell Cain

Our Boutique

OUR BOUTIQUE IS OPEN DAILY.
WE HAVE A WONDERFUL VARIETY
OF ITEMS FOR GIFTS OR A LITTLE
SOMETHING FOR YOURSELF.

Special Occasions

At the Ivy House we have a special meal planned for every occasion. Birthdays, Girls Night Out, Mother's Day, Valentine's Day, Thanksgiving, and Christmas.

See you soon!

Valentines Day

Mother's Day

Thanksgiving

Christmas

123

Ivy House —
Thank you for
the food, the
great, inspirational
signs and the
basket! I so
appreciate your
support
God Bless —
Sarah Palin
'08

Another addition is The Garden Room, "the favorite of the customers." This room was originally our side porch that we used to drape with old quilts and add heaters in the winter. For extra seating, we have enclosed this room with lots of French-paned windows. The sun comes in through the windows and it's very airy, which draws the customers in. The Red Room was the last dining room we added. This room is very special because it was once the original portico for the old house. We raised the floor and enclosed the walls, leaving the old columns showing through, which gives an antique feel to the room. We painted the walls a deep red and wallpapered in black and gold toile. The setting is very romantic. My dear friend, Charlene Whitehurst, and her daughter, Stephanie, are like little fairies, popping in to spruce up and decorate the rooms for the different seasons. Although we have taken each room and given them all unique themes, some customers have the misconception that we are a tea room or a fine dining restaurant. That couldn't be farther from the truth. Our menu and plate portions are nothing you will find in a tea house, and we welcome everyone to our casual restaurant.

The Ivy House has won many awards, including being one of "THE TOP 500 PLACES TO EAT in the State of Florida" for the past six years. We just received the newest one for 2008. Not only do we run the restaurant, but we also have a full catering service.

GOVENOR SARAH PALIN wrote this note to us after The Ivy House catered an event for her on November 11, 2008. "The Road to Victory Rally." It was such an honor for us to be a part of this event. We had met Sarah twice prior this Event.

SHE IS AMAZING AND TRULY LOVES THE LORD.

The most spectacular catering job was in New York.
We were flown in on a private jet by our friend, Becky Ray,
formerly Becky Thomas, to cater her stallion show.

The best part of it all was when all the northerners tasted
our food, they were amazed! They said they could not believe the
flavor and how pretty the food was. Some said they felt like
they had died and gone to heaven.

A Little Southern
COOKING NEVER HURT ANYONE.

From 2002 to 2007, we catered in Kentucky four times
a year for two to three weeks at a time.
We catered at Keeneland for the thoroughbred industry,
cooking breakfast and lunch for groups anywhere
from 90 to 425 people. On top of that, we would be required
to fix between 20 to 60 gallons
of homemade soup each day. The job was tough, but taught
us a lot about catering for mass quantities.

Evelyn, MiMi, Waica 2006

Through jobs like this, we have met wonderful friends like Thelma and Russ Johns of Lexington. They were like our family away from home. Mrs. Thelma helped us with our catering in Kentucky and has been a Godsend many times. Some of you might have met her, or at least tasted some of her yummy chocolates. She has come down for our Christmas Open House and set up on the porch to sell her wonderful chocolate-covered apples and handmade chocolate candies. They are precious people, definitely friends for life.

Everyone had encouraged me to start The Ivy House because I loved to cook and was always having lots of company and family. Everyone, including one of my biggest supporters, Charles Webb, who said, "You need to open a restaurant!" I told them that I would love to, but that Williston was just a small town. I continued to hesitate for some years, and then one day I attended a womens conference. The guest speaker told me that God was going to use me in a special way to touch peoples lives.

I SAID TO MYSELF,

"I can't do anything but cook!"

That is when the door opened up for the business and it has been rewarding ever since. Only by the grace of God has our little restaurant flourished on a side street in such a small town like Williston. He has sent us wonderful customers that come from all over to visit us, many of which have become great friends over the years. I hope as you read through my cookbook and try some of our delicious recipes, that you can experience the love and joy that we have received.

MAY GOD CONTINUE TO BLESS YOU AND YOUR FAMILY.

Our *Family*

128

...*Grace & Peace*

FROM OUR FAMILY TO YOURS.

Main Dishes,
Meat, Poultry & Seafood

Southern Pork Chops WITH APPLES

6 pork chops
1 tablespoon vegetable oil
1 cup sour cream
1 can cream of mushroom soup
1/2 cup brown sugar
4-6 tart apples, sliced
Salt and pepper to taste

- **In skillet, heat oil and brown pork chops on both sides.**
- Mix soup and sour cream together, spread 1/2 amount in a 9 x 13 baking dish.
- Dip apples in brown sugar to coat and place on top of soup mixture.
- **Place browned chops on top of the apples.**
- **Spread remaining soup mixture over pork chops.**
- Cover and bake at 325º for 1 hour.

YOU WILL HAVE A NICE GRAVY WHEN THE DISH COMES OUT OF THE OVEN.
IT IS DELICIOUS SERVED WITH WILD RICE:
1 1/2 CUPS RICE, 1/2 CUP WILD RICE, 4-4 1/2 CUPS WATER.
MIX AND COOK FOR 20 -25 MINUTES. SALT TO TASTE.

SERVE TOPPED WITH THE GRAVY.

Yummy!

My husband, what an encourager you were. I miss all your compliments,
your kind unexpected gestures and your unconditional love.
Your faith in me, gave me the strength to do anything.
I miss you dearly. I know you were so excited about this cookbook, I'm just sorry you
were not here to see it or promote it. I know you would have been so proud.

"My Hero," I Love You!
Lil "Joe"

Thanks for always being there
Dad, standing by me.
I Love You, Myra

I will miss your sweet chuckle,
I love you. Micala

You made up for everything,
I missed out on with my Daddy.
I Love You Forever & Ever,
Waica

Thanks for your on time,
wisdom and great jokes.
I love you! Love, Michael

I will drink enough milk for the
both of us. I love you, Ellizabeth

I will miss your funny faces that
made me always laugh, all the boiled
peanuts and all the ice cream surprises,
Love, Lil' Art

I miss our long late night talks
and our lemon & vinegar parties.
Love Your Baby Girl, "Evelyn"

Best story teller ever!
I will miss you, Love, Zack

First and last man I ever loved,
I will always cherish the times
I had with you.
Love your Monkey, Ann

I will miss you telling me what
back roads to travel and that
you never met a stranger. Art

I will always miss you not sitting on the
front porch at the Ivy House, you will
always be "My Hero." Love Alesha

Papa, we will miss our
marshmellow treats.
Michael, McKenzie & Braxton

I will miss you spoiling me
and sneaking me treats.
Love, Dylan

PaPa's Sip of Fun & Laughter

When growing up, our girls always had their friends over and Ann, Myra and Evelyn would fix this concoction (Papa's recipe). In spite of much protesting, coughing, choking, and carrying on, their friends would eventually sip it down. Would you believe that some of them became addicted and learned to love it, too? Now they enjoy reminiscing about these good times.

Papa and Evelyn

Squeezing Lemons for Their Special Drink

This recipe has been passed down to my grandchildren and great-grandchildren. They love it too. In fact, when we talk about it or think about it, we get that twinge right under the ear lobe on the jaw.

We were desperate for crushed ice. We would wrap the ice in a tea towel and beat it with a hammer, this was before we had our crushed ice machine.

WARNING:
JUST SIP, DON'T DRINK! MAY CAUSE CHOKING.
(HA! HA! -- NO REALLY!)

2 tablespoon red wine vinegar
2 tablespoon fresh squeezed lemon juice
1/8 cup crushed ice (a must)
Salt to taste

- **Mix all ingredients well.**
- Serve in a small crystal glass or snifter. Enjoy!
- **You can also add a little orange juice to the mixture for an alternative taste.**

133

Papa's LOGGING HASH

1 large can of dried corned beef (not hash)
1 can lima beans, drained and rinsed
1 can diced tomatoes
1 large onion, chopped
1 large baking potato, sliced like home fries
1 can chicken noodle soup or 1 can chicken broth
2 tablespoons vegetable oil

- **Stir - fry potato and onion in the vegetable oil.**
- In a stock pot add all ingredients together.
- **Bring to a boil over medium heat.**
- Then turn down the heat and simmer for 20-30 minutes, allowing the flavors to blend.
- **Serve in a soup bowl with Saltine crackers or cornbread and maybe a couple dashes of hot sauce. Yummy!**

In the log woods, Freddie cooked this hash in a big black pot over an open fire,
and fed all the men. He gave them Saltine crackers, but at home, we make good ole' cornbread.
Our whole family loves it. Papa made it for us quite often in the colder months of the year.

It was comical to watch him make it because he just threw it all together
in a big pot and it came out tasting great as always.
We have all tried to tackle the soup at some point or another,
BUT IT NEVER TASTES LIKE PAPA'S.
I GUESS HE GAVE IT THAT SPECIAL TOUCH.
I HOPE YOUR FAMILY LIKES IT AS MUCH AS MINE DOES.

Freddie and his daddy, Newton Hale, bought our cooker in the 60's
from B.E. Brice Sawmill in Bronson,
Florida. Mr. Brice and his brother designed and manufactured them.
Mr. Brice's daughters still have the sawmill and have
BK Cypress Log Homes in Bronson, Fl.

There's no way of knowing how many hams, loins and chickens
FREDDIE HAS SMOKED AND CARRIED
to our friends and neighbors in the three surrounding counties.

THIS IS A TRADITION
THAT WE STILL DO IN MEMORY OF PAPA.

Freddie's Famous SMOKED MEAT

OTHER OPTIONS:

- **1 fresh ham or cured ham, (Freddie's favorite), fresh pork loin, or 6 chickens cut into quarters.**

- Select the meat of choice and completely cover with black pepper and salt to taste.

- **Smoke in a cooker 6- 8 hours on 200° or until meat is well done and tender.**

- Slice or cut up and serve with your favorite barbecue sauce.

DON'T SALT THE RED HAM BECAUSE IT'S CURED.
We call in our meat order and get the meat man to debone and skin the hams.
Make sure to tell them to tie them up tight so they won't fall apart while smoking.

Baked Pork Chops WITH CREAM GRAVY

6 pork chops
1 cup self-rising flour
1/2 cup milk
Salt and pepper to taste
1 egg, beaten

- **Salt and pepper the chops.**
- Mix the milk and egg.
- **Dip pork chops in egg mixture and then into the flour.**
- Place the chops on a heavily greased baking pan.
- **Bake in a 350° oven for 30 minutes.**
- Turn the chops over and continue baking 10-15 minutes more and serve.

Cream Gravy

1/2 cup self-rising flour
1 cup canned cream (evaporated milk)
Salt and pepper
1 cup water

- **Pour drippings from baking pan into a skillet and add flour, cream and water.**
- Mix well and bring to a boil, stirring constantly.
- **You may add more water or milk to make the right consistency.**
- Serve with homemade whipped potatoes or rice.

My grandson, Michael, loves these pork chops. He said,
"MIMI, I COULD EAT THEM EVERY DAY!
It was also his Daddy's favorite. We would always cook a big supper every night.
I would cook 15-20 pork chops for my boys.

My Michael has a beautiful wife, Brittany, and they have three beautiful
children - Michael III, McKenzie, and Braxton.

SMOKED PICNIC HAM *For Pulled Pork*

1 picnic ham
3-4 Coca Colas

- **Place the ham in a baking pan.**
- Pour Coke over the ham, enough to provide 1 to 2 inches of Cola in the pan.
- **Cover and bake in a 350° oven 15 minutes per pound or until so tender the meat falls apart. After the ham is done, remove the skin and fat and pull meat into shreds.**
- Save the bones and juice to season vegetables or soups.

FRIED COUNTRY *Ham Slices & Red-Eye Gravy*

2 (12-oz.) packages of country ham slices
1 cup hot coffee or water

- **Soak ham in warm water 15 minutes; drain.**
- Brown ham on both sides over medium heat and remove to warm platter.
- **Discard drippings from skillet. Pour hot coffee into skillet. Stir and scrap ham particles from skillet, mixing with the coffee. Serve with hot biscuits, cheese grits, and fried eggs.**

Country Beef Wellington

1 1/2 pounds ground round steak
2 slices bread
2 cups canned cream (evaporated milk)
1 chunk cheddar cheese, cut into large pieces
1 medium onion, finely chopped
1 medium green bell pepper, finely chopped
1 can diced tomatoes
1 tablespoon flour
1 unbaked pie crust
Salt and pepper to taste

- **Mix the ground steak, salt and pepper and the bread that has been soaked in 1/2 cup cream.**
- Roll into balls about the size of a muffin cup and place in a baking pan.
- **Push a hole in each ball and place a piece of cheese (about a tablespoon size) into it, squeezing top to cover the cheese.**
- Cut pie crust into small round circles and place on top of each ball.
- **Bake 325° for 30 minutes.**
- Mix tomatoes, onions, bell pepper, and remaining milk and pour around the balls. This makes a perfect tomato gravy.
- **Continue baking for another 30 minutes or until crust is golden brown.**

Homemade
WHIPPED POTATOES
ARE A MUST WITH THIS MEAT ENTREE!

Beef Pot Pie

1 pound sirloin beef tips, cut into cubes
4 tablespoons self-rising flour
1/2 cup canned cream (evaporated milk)
4 cups beef broth
1/3 cup extra virgin olive oil
1 large onion, finely chopped
1 cup frozen English peas
1 cup fresh carrots, finely chopped
Salt and pepper to taste
2 large unbaked pie shells

- **Brown, then simmer the beef cubes until tender; set aside.**

- In a sauce pan, over medium heat, blend the olive oil and flour until smooth.

- **Add beef broth. (You can use the broth from cooking the beef.) Add cream, onion, peas, and carrots. Cook until well blended and thickened.**

- Fold in the cooked beef cubes and pour into one of the unbaked pie shells.

- **Cut the second pie shell into strips and place on top of beef mixture.**

- Bake in a 350º oven for 40-45 minutes, until crust is golden brown.

POT PIE

Roast Meat Loaf

1 1/2 pounds ground round steak
1/2 pound ground pork sausage
3 eggs, beaten
1/4 teaspoon nutmeg
1/4 cup milk
1/4 cup sour cream
1 cup soft white bread crumbs
1 medium onion, finely chopped
1 can cream of mushroom soup
1/2 cup brown sugar
1/2 cup vinegar
Salt and pepper to taste
1/2 cup ketchup
6 slices bacon

- **Mix beef, pork, eggs, salt, pepper and nutmeg until well blended.**
- Combine milk, sour cream and bread crumbs. Allow to set for about 5 minutes before adding the mushroom soup and onion.
- **Add mixture to meat and lightly mix until blended.**
- Turn into a shallow baking pan.
- **Moisten hands with water and shape meat mixture into a flat loaf about 9 x 13.**
- Place bacon slices on top and bake at 350º for 45 minutes.
- **Mix ketchup, brown sugar, and vinegar; cover top and sides of meat loaf.**
- Bake 30 minutes longer.
- **Garnish with freshly chopped parsley.**

MY FAMILY'S *Favorite Sirloin Tips*

2 pounds sirloin beef tips or beef stew
1/4 cup vegetable oil
2 slices bacon, cut into small pieces
1/2 small bag baby carrots
1 large onion, finely chopped
1 tablespoon garlic, minced
1 bay leaf
3 cups water
1/2 cup self-rising flour
1/2 cup canned cream (evaporated milk)
Salt and pepper to taste

- **In a large Dutch oven, brown beef tips in oil and bacon.**

- Stir in onions and cook until caramelized.

- **Take out the meat and onions and set aside.**

- Add flour to Dutch oven and brown in the meat drippings and bacon grease.

- **After getting the flour good and brown, remove the flour as much as you can and set aside.**

- Return the meat and onions to the Dutch oven and cover the meat with water. Then cover and simmer until meat is tender. Add your carrots, minced garlic, and 1 bay leaf and simmer until carrots are tender.

- **Bring to low heat.**

- Add brown flour to meat, 1/2 cup canned cream, salt and pepper, and remaining water if it's too thick.

- **Blend all together. Continue cooking on low heat until flour has thickened and flavors are blended and consistency is smooth.**

Our Sunday
Dinner Best Roast

1 eye of round roast (about 3 pounds)
1 large pork tenderloin
1 cup flour
1/2 cup vegetable oil
4 slices lean white bacon
Salt and pepper to taste

- **In a Dutch oven, fry bacon in vegetable oil.**
- Remove the bacon; salt and pepper each roast and roll in the flour to coat well.
- **Pour bacon grease and vegetable oil over the flavored roast and rub it in.**
- Place the two roasts side by side in the pan and brown well on all sides.
- **Add enough hot water to surround about half of the roast.**
- Cover and bake at 300° for 2 hours or until meat is very tender.

YOU WILL HAVE A DELICIOUS
GRAVY WITH THIS ROAST.
REMOVE THE ROAST TO A PLATTER, AND STIR THE GRAVY UNTIL SMOOTH.
YOU MIGHT WANT TO ADD A LITTLE HOT WATER TO MAKE YOUR GRAVY PERFECT.

THE FLAVORS IN THIS MEAL ARE INCREDIBLE WHEN YOU COOK THE PORK
AND EYE OF THE ROUND TOGETHER
AND SERVE IT OVER HOMEMADE MASHED POTATOES.

I HAVE TO SAY, BEST MEAL EVER!

SHRIMP

Shrimp Scampi

Serves 6

36 large shrimp
1 stick butter
1/3 cup vegetable oil
1 tablespoon chopped garlic
1/2 teaspoon paprika

- **Shell and devein shrimp.**
- Combine butter, oil and garlic in medium hot skillet.
- **Add 12 shrimp at a time to the hot butter mixture and saute 2-3 minutes, until shrimp turns pink.**
- Serve on a bed of savory rice and garnish with paprika and chopped parsley or serve over a Filet Mignon from our signature recipe.

Photo on page 8

Crab Meat Casserole

1 pound crab meat
1/4 pound Ritz crackers, crushed
1 onion, minced
2 cloves garlic, minced
1/2 pint whipping cream
1 stick butter

- **Brown onions in 1/2 stick of butter, add cream and garlic to onions mixing well.**
- Add crab meat and 1/2 crushed crackers. Mix and pour into a buttered casserole dish.
- **Add remaining crackers over the top. Melt 1/2 butter and pour over the crackers.**
- Bake in a 350° oven for 15-20 minutes until bubbly.

CRAB MEAT

Baked Hot Chicken Salad

6 boneless chicken breasts
1 cup rice, cooked
I medium onion, chopped
2 cups celery, finely chopped
I can cream of chicken soup
1/2 cup mayonnaise
2 tablespoons lemon juice
1 1/2 cups slivered almonds
1 tablespoon paprika
Salt and pepper to taste

- **Cook the chicken until tender.**
- Salt and pepper the chicken and cut into bite-size pieces.
- **Cook rice as directed; 1 cup rice, 2 cups water, 1 teaspoon salt**
- Mix chicken, rice, soup, mayonnaise, onion, celery and lemon juice in a bowl.
- **Pour into a 9 x 13 baking dish and bake for 30 minutes.**
- Sprinkle with almonds about halfway through cooking.
- **Remove from oven and sprinkle with paprika.**

DUMPLINGS

Chicken & Dumplings

1 roasting hen
2 packages frozen dumplings
1 cup canned cream (evaporated milk)
Chicken broth
Salt and pepper to taste

- **Boil hen in 2 quarts of water.** "De-bone, de-skin, de-everything" **and cut the chicken into bite-size pieces.**

- In a Dutch oven, bring broth back to a boil; then drop dumplings, one at a time, into the boiling liquid.

- **Cook as directed on dumpling package.**

- Add the canned cream during the last 5 minutes of cooking. Gently fold in chicken pieces.

- **You can add a little more hot water to the broth to make the right consistency.**

Polynesian Chicken

3 boneless chicken breasts
1/2 cup self-rising flour
1 egg, slightly beaten
1/2 cup water
2 teaspoons sesame seeds
2 cups vegetable oil
1 (16-oz.) can apricot halves, drained (pineapple chunks may be substituted)
1 (6-oz.) package frozen pea pods, strings off
3/4 cup sweet and sour sauce
Salt and pepper to taste
Hot cooked white rice

- **Cut chicken breasts into nugget-size pieces; salt and pepper.**
- Mix flour, sesame seeds, egg and water to make a batter.
- **Dip chicken into batter and fry in vegetable oil heated to 325° until golden brown.**
- Combine apricots, pea pods and sauce. Cook over medium heat until thoroughly heated and bubbly.
- **Serve on a platter with white rice, lay chicken on top of the rice and pour hot sauce over the combination.**

THIS IS DELICIOUS AND MAKES A BEAUTIFUL PRESENTATION.

Southern Chicken Pot Pie

3 pounds fryer chicken, boiled and de-boned
4 tablespoons self-rising flour
1/2 stick butter
3 cups chicken broth
1 cup canned cream (evaporated milk)
1 large onion, finely chopped
1 cup frozen green peas
1 cup fresh carrots, chopped
Salt and pepper to taste
2 unbaked pie shells, 9" deep dish

- **In a sauce pan, melt butter and mix in flour until smooth.**
- Add chicken broth (strained) made from boiling the chicken.
- **Add milk, frozen peas, carrots and onion.**
- Stir and cook until well blended and thickened.
- **Add a little water, if needed, to achieve the right consistency.**
- Fold in the chicken and pour mixture into one of the unbaked pie shells.
- **Cut the second pie shell into strips and place on top of the chicken mixture.**
- Bake until crust is golden brown, approximately 35-45 minutes at 350°.

Easy Baked *Naked Chicken*

- **1 fryer, cut into quarters**
- Salt and pepper to taste.
- **Place chicken in a shallow baking pan; skin side up.**
- Bake at 375° for 40-45 minutes until golden brown.
- **Serve on a platter.**

SIMPLE IS SOMETIMES BETTER.
SO EASY, SO GOOD!

Baked Chicken WITH PARMESAN SAUCE

1 fryer, cut up
Salt and pepper to taste

- **Salt and pepper the chicken and place on a shallow baking pan.**
- Cook 45 minutes at 375° or until nice and brown.

PARMESAN SAUCE

3 tablespoons plain flour
3 tablespoons butter
1 cup chicken stock
1 tablespoon minced onion
1 cup canned cream (evaporated milk)
1/2 cup freshly grated parmesan cheese
1/4 cup white grape juice (my substitution for white wine)
Salt and pepper to taste

- **In a sauce pan, combine flour and butter.**
- Cook 10 minutes, stirring until smooth, but do not brown.
- **Add chicken stock, onion, cream, cheese, salt and pepper.**
- Cook 5 minutes. Serve over baked chicken.

Southern Pecan Baked Chicken

Yield: 8 servings

8 chicken breasts
1 stick butter (melted)
1 egg, slightly beaten

1 cup self-rising flour
1 cup chopped pecans (not to fine)
Salt and pepper to taste
1/2 cup olive oil
2 cups bread crumbs finely processed

- **Combine flour, bread crumbs, chopped pecans, salt, and pepper.**

- Dip chicken in melted butter, then egg and then roll in flour. Place them on a greased sheet pan.

- **Top with a few more chopped pecans and drizzle the olive oil over each chicken breast and bake at 350° for 30 minutes.**

Praline Sauce

1 1/4 cups light brown sugar
3/4 cup evaporated milk
1 tbsp. butter

1/2 tsp. vanilla
1/4 cup chopped pecans

- In a saucepan over low heat combine brown sugar, evaporated milk, and butter.

- Cook and stir praline sauce until sauce is smooth and syrupy, about 5 minutes.

- Stir in vanilla extract and pecans.

- Drizzle sauce over pecan chicken, just before serving.

This recipe is wonderful. We fix it sometimes for our Mother's Day lunch at the Ivy House. We serve it with homemade mashed potatoes, green beans, candied sweet potato and garden salad.

SO DELICIOUS!!!

Baked Poppy Seed Chicken

6 boneless chicken breasts
1 can cream of chicken soup
1 cup sour cream
1 tablespoon poppy seed
1 sleeve Ritz crackers, crushed
1 stick butter
Salt and pepper to taste

- **Place chicken breast in a greased 9x13 pan.**
- Mix soup and sour cream with the poppy seed and pour over chicken.
- **Melt butter and mix with crushed Ritz crackers and set aside.**
- Bake at 350° for 45 minutes.
- **About 20 minutes before baking is complete, spread the buttered cracker crumbs on top of the dish and continue cooking until crumbs are toasted and golden brown.**

Chicken Taco Salad

4 boneless chicken breasts
1 package taco seasoning
1/2 cup water
1 head iceberg lettuce, chopped
1 head romaine lettuce, chopped
1/2 cup green onions, chopped
1/2 cup black olives, chopped
1/2 cup shredded cheddar cheese
1 cup kidney beans, rinsed and drained
1 (1-oz.) bottle Catalina dressing
1 medium bag Doritos, crushed
Salt and pepper to taste

- **Boil chicken and cut into bite-size pieces.**
- Mix taco seasoning and water in a small sauce pan, cooking on medium heat, until it comes to a boil. Mix well and allow to cool.
- **Mix chicken and taco mixture.**
- Combine lettuce, onions, olives, cheese and beans.
- **Then fold in the chicken and Doritos.**
- Pour in the bottled dressing and toss lightly.

IT IS TRULY DELICIOUS.
Nice cool salad on a hot summer day.

MiMi's Open-Faced
CHICKEN SANDWICHES

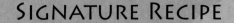

6 boneless chicken breasts, boiled and chopped
1/2 cup onion, chopped
2 cups sliced mushrooms
1/4 teaspoon thyme
1 cup mayonnaise
4 hard boiled eggs, chopped
1/2 cup celery, chopped
Salt and pepper to taste
6 English muffins, split and toasted
12 slices American cheese
1 can cream of chicken soup
1 cup sour cream

- **Mix the chicken with onions, mushrooms, thyme, mayonnaise, eggs and celery.**

- Place the toasted muffins in a baking dish and pour the chicken mixture over the muffins.

- **Top each with sliced cheese. Mix the chicken soup and sour cream and cover muffins with the mixture.**

- Bake at 350° for 45 minutes.

- **Separate and serve as individual open-faced sandwiches.**

Skillet Chicken

4 chicken breasts
1/2 stick butter
2 tablespoons oil
1/2 cup sliced mushrooms
1/4 cup chicken broth
1/4 cup white grape juice
1 cup canned cream (evaporated milk)
1 teaspoon fresh lemon juice
2 tablespoons fresh parsley, chopped
1 tablespoon rosemary

- **Slightly brown chicken in a large skillet with the butter and oil; add mushrooms and saute.**

- Add broth, juice, cream, lemon juice and rosemary.

- **Cover and let simmer until chicken is tender, about 20 minutes.**

- Sprinkle with the parsley to garnish.

CHICKEN

My grandson, Little Joe, just loves this dish.
IT'S ONE OF HIS FAVORITE MEALS.
And my other boy, Andy, says the secret is a lot of salt and pepper, and he's right.
There's nothing better than good ole' seasoned chicken.

Aunt Nettie's PURLOW

1 nice, big, fat hen
4 cups rice, uncooked
1 kitchen spoon black pepper
  (McCormick's is the right flavor and hotness and won't turn the rice black.)

- **Boil in a large amount of water until tender. Remove the skin and de-bone chicken, then chop into small pieces.**
- In a large pot, put 13 cups of the chicken stock and bring to a boil.
- **Add the rice and boil 10 minutes, stirring constantly.**
- Then reduce heat to simmer, stirring occasionally, for approximately 20 minutes, then fold in chicken. (Have extra boiling, salted water on the side , add to chicken and rice if needed.)
- **Serve heaping helpings and enjoy.**

PURLOW

Griffin Southern Chicken Rice
"PURLOW"

My sister, Nettie, married N.E. Griffin in 1941. They lived in an apartment next to N.E.'s mother and father, Alice and Arthur Griffin. When they had their family gatherings, the main special meal was Purlow cooked in a black iron wash pot outside, only after it was cleaned out of course. They would mostly boil the old hens and roosters that were on the farm until they were good and tender. Probably four or five hens at a time. For every hen, they cooked 4 cups of rice, and of course the secret seasoning was McCormick black pepper. It was a must to create the perfect Purlow. McCormick pepper is just the right coarse and just the right peppery taste. Then you need to add some salt to taste. Family gatherings at the Griffin house would not have been the same without the Purlow. Unexpected company was always welcomed. They would just add a little more pepper to the black iron pot to make it stretch. After the laughing, eating and reminiscing was done, that old black pot had to get back to its other chores like boiling clothes, making homemade lye soap, cooking the fat meat to make lard for the year and boiling peanuts. There is a lot that has changed since then, we have come a long way, but one thing that won't ever change is the love and memories that come from making that good ole' Purlow. I would love to know how many pots of Purlow Nettie has made for children, grandchildren, and great-grandchildren.

SHE WAS A SPECIAL LADY AND A GREAT COOK.
WE ALL MISS HER DEARLY.

Baked Chicken & Rice

1 large fryer, cut up
2 cups rice
1 can cream of chicken soup
1 can cream of mushroom soup
2 cups milk
2 cups water
Salt and pepper to taste

- **Mix rice, chicken soup, mushroom soup, milk, water, salt and pepper.**
- Pour into roasting pan. Place chicken pieces on top of rice mixture.
- **Bake uncovered for 1 - 1 1/4 hours. Add more milk or water if rice becomes a little dry.**

SIMPLE TO MAKE,
BUT DELICIOUS TO EAT.

MAHI-MAHI

Caribbean Mahi-Mahi

1/3 cup lime juice
3 tablespoons soy sauce
1 tablespoon vegetable oil
1/4 teaspoon ground red pepper
1/4 teaspoon garlic powder
1/4 teaspoon ground coriander
1/4 teaspoon cinnamon
1 1/4 teaspoon dried mint
1 1/2 pounds Mahi-Mahi filets

- **Combine the first 8 ingredients in a jar and shake to mix.**
- Place filets in glass baking dish and pour marinade over fish.
- **Cover and refrigerate 30 minutes to 1 hour.**
- Broil 5-6 inches from broiler on greased rack, turning halfway through broiling.
- **Allow 10 minutes for each inch of thickness of filets.**

Shrimp & Crab Meat SALAD OVER PINK RICE

Pink Rice (recipe below)

1/2 cup olives, chopped
2 tablespoons sweet pickle relish
3 heaping tablespoons mayonnaise
1 can crab meat, drained
1 pound boiled shrimp, peeled and chopped into small pieces.
3-4 boiled eggs
1/4 cup celery, finely chopped
1/4 cup pimento, chopped
1/4 cup green onions, finely chopped

- **Mix rice, olives, pickle relish, mayonnaise, celery, pimento and onions.**
- Fold in crab meat and shrimp, along with the eggs.
- **Pour rice onto a large platter and put the shrimp and crab salad on top.**
- Garnish with celery leaves, grape tomatoes, and lemon wedges.

Pink Rice

2 cups white rice
2 sliced beets

- **Cook the rice according to package directions, and adding two slices of beets to the boiling water.**
- Remove beets when cooking is complete.
- **This makes a nice, pale pink rice that compliments the dish.**

YOU MAY ALSO USE WHITE RICE INSTEAD
OF THE PINK IN THIS DISH IF YOU PREFER.

Grilled Salmon WITH BASIL MUSTARD CRUST

3 tablespoons Dijon mustard
3 tablespoons fresh basil, minced
1 1/2 teaspoons olive oil
1 pound skinless salmon filets

- **Mix mustard, basil and olive oil.**
- Spread on both sides of the filets.
- **Refrigerate until ready to cook.**
- Spray grill and grill filets 5 minutes on each side.
- **Let stand covered with foil. Cut into 4 pieces.**

Salmon Burgers

1 pound boneless, skinless salmon filet, chopped fine
2 tablespoons bread crumbs
1 tablespoon dijon mustard
1 tablespoon onion, minced
2 teaspoons lemon juice
1/2 teaspoon garlic, minced
Salt and pepper to taste
4 hamburger buns
Mayonnaise or tartar sauce to taste

- **Mix all ingredients and shape into four patties.**
- Place on a plate and refrigerate until well chilled.
- **Grill two minutes on each side over medium coals, turning once.**
- Serve on toasted, buttered buns with mayonnaise or tartar sauce.

Salmon Patties

1/2 can salmon "de-boned, de-skin, de-everything"
1 egg
1 medium onion, finely chopped
Self-rising flour
Vegetable oil

- **Combine 1/2 can of salmon, egg and onion.**
- Add enough flour to bind the ingredients together.
- **Shape into patties and fry in a small amount of vegetable oil until browned.**

GRANDMA RAY'S QUICK
Salmon & Rice Purlow

1/2 can salmon,
1 cups white rice (Uncle Ben's converted)
4 cups water
1 stick butter
Salt and Peper to taste

- **Cook rice, salmon and butter.**
- Stir Lightly.
- **Serve with salmon patties.**

MAIN DISHES - MEATS, POULTRY & SEAFOOD

Sauces

Dylan's Dippin' Sauce

1 cup mayonnaise

10 tablespoons ketchup

4 tablespoons Sticky Finger BBQ sauce, "Carolina Classic"

1/2 teaspoon salt

1/2 teaspoon pepper

1 teaspoon honey dijon mustard

1 teaspoon Louisiana hot sauce

This recipe was made up by my seven year old great-grandson Dylan, Waica's son.
He whips this sauce up when he and his dad, Zack, fry up a batch of venison and taters.
Waica said she came home one day and he had a little bit of everything pulled out of the fridge
and he was stirring up something. She said, "Whatcha' doing, Bud?"
And he said, "I'm making my sauce," and looked at her like, "this ain't my first rodeo."

Come to find out, Dylan had made this sauce several other times when
Waica was out of town working.

HIS SAUCE IS REALLY GOOD.

It's great on any meats and fried potatoes.
Our favorites are fried venison, pork, turkey, chicken, and

YUMMY ON FRIED SHRIMP.

Creamy White Sauce

1 can evaporated milk
1 cup milk
4 tablespoons butter
4 tablespoons self-rising flour

- **In a sauce pan, melt the butter and stir in the flour until smooth.**
- Add the two milks, gradually stirring until the sauce is thickened, about 1 minute.

CREAMY WHITE SAUCE

The canned cream gives this sauce a real creamy taste. It can be used for many creations.
Cut up chicken or turkey pieces and add to the sauce to make

A NICE TOPPING FOR TOAST.

Add cheese to the sauce and serve over baked potatoes.
Use this sauce and your own creativity to add variety to your meals.

Art (Evelyn's Husband) says I can't make anything without canned cream (evaporated milk) and butter.
So when he does the shopping he loads my fridge and pantry
full of butter and canned cream (evaporated milk)- **It's a must!!!!**

SO GOOD!

Creamy Mustard Sauce

Yield: 1 cup

1 cup sour cream
1 tablespoon dijon mustard
1 teaspoon prepared mustard
6 dashes hot pepper sauce

- **Combine all ingredients in a small bowl.**
- Mix well.

EXCEPTIONALLY GOOD TO USE WITH CRAB BURGERS,
COOKED SHRIMP, AND BAKED FISH.

Horseradish Sauce

1 cup sour cream
1 teaspoon rice vinegar
1 dash tabasco sauce
1 small onion, finely grated
1 teaspoon horseradish
1 pinch sugar
Salt to taste
Yellow mustard to taste

- **Combine all ingredients in a small bowl and mix well.**
- Refrigerate.

This is the perfect accompaniment for that delicious Prime Rib. For variety, try making this sauce with a rice vinegar that has been seasoned with basil and oregano.

DIFFERENT AND GOOD.

LIME-RED PEPPER Hollandaise Sauce

1/2 cup butter
1 tablespoon water
2 tablespoons fresh lime juice
3 egg yolks, beaten
1 teaspoon grated lime zest
1/4 teaspoon cayenne pepper

- **Mix all ingredients until well blended.**
- In saucepan over medium heat, bring to gentle boil intil creamy.

THE MORE FINELY GRATED THE ZEST, THE STRONGER THE LIME FLAVOR.

Lemon Dijon Butter

1 stick butter
2 teaspoons fresh lemon juice
2 teaspoons minced parsley
2 tablespoons dijon mustard
Salt and pepper to taste

- **Combine the butter, lemon juice, parsley, salt and pepper in a small bowl.**
- Add the mustard and mix well. Cover and refrigerate until serving time.

LEMON
DIJON BUTTER

SERVE OVER BAKED FISH OR BAKED CHICKEN.
IT PROVIDES THAT SPECIAL
FINISHING TOUCH TO YOUR ENTR'EE.

Pesto Sauce

Yield: 3/4 cup

1 cup fresh spinach
1 cup fresh basil leaves, packed
1/3 cup olive oil
1/3 cup pine nuts or walnuts
1/3 cup parmesan cheese
1 clove garlic, peeled
1/4 teaspoon salt

- **Combine all ingredients in a blender and process until smooth.**

PESTO SAUCE

SERVE PESTO WITH FRESH BAKED BREAD
OR SERVE TOSSED WITH COOKED PASTA
TO MAKE A WONDERFUL SIDE DISH.

Bread & Rolls

OUR SIGNATURE RECIPE

Ivy House Corny Cornbread

1 box Jiffy cornbread mix
1 cup cream corn
4 eggs, beaten
1 cup onion, chopped
1 cup shredded cheddar cheese
1 stick butter, melted

- **Gently mix all ingredients and pour into a sprayed 9 x 13 baking pan.**
- Bake at 350º - 400º until golden brown, about 30-40 minutes.

Enjoy it!

THIS RECIPE IS FOR ALL YOU SPECIAL PEOPLE
WHO HAVE EATEN
THIS DELICIOUS CORNBREAD
AT THE IVY HOUSE AND HAVE LOVED IT.

Hoe Cake Biscuits BAKED IN BLACK SKILLET

3 teaspoons bacon grease
1 cup buttermilk, add pinch of baking soda
2 cups self-rising flour
1/2 cup cooking oil
1 tablespoon sugar

- **Grease bottom and sides of black skillet with bacon grease.**
- In a mixing bowl, add flour and sugar. Make a hole and pour in buttermilk and add vegetable oil.
- **Gently stir to make a soft dough, pulling flour in from sides to form a ball.**
- Heat the skillet until hot. Flour fingers and knead ball until you can pick it up.
- **Gently put into skillet and pat down the dough until it fills the pan.**
- Bake at 450º for 15-20 minutes or until golden brown.
- **Serve piping hot!**

THIS MAKES A GOOD OLD - TIMEY DESSERT
served with lots of butter and homemade cane syrup.
You can also make a cornbread hot cake by substituting
1 cup self-rising cornmeal for 1 cup of the flour.

We love this with our lima bean supper.
My brother, Lawton Ray, relished this hot cake
and loved to drag it in cane syrup for a special treat after supper.

So good!

MiMi's Melt-Away Mini Biscuits

2 cups self-rising flour
2 cups whipping cream
1/2 cup butter, melted

- **You will need to use miniature muffin tins for these biscuits.**

- Brush a small amount of melted butter into each muffin cup.

- **Gently mix flour and whipping cream until blended.**

- Spoon mixture into muffin cups 2/3 full. Spoon remaining melted butter on top.

- **Bake in a preheated 400° oven for 15 minutes or until golden brown.**

- Makes 24 biscuits.

Ivy House Yeast Rolls

1 package frozen yeast rolls
1 stick butter, melted

- Let rolls thaw about 30 minutes or until soft. Roll each dough ball into melted butter to coat really well.

- **Pull the dough out flat about the size of a jar top. Fold 1/3 of a side over and shape out flat again and allow to rise.**

- Bake at 450° 10-15 minutes or until golden brown.

Sometimes for parties, we put a teaspoon of jam or marmalade under the fold before baking.
THESE ARE REALLY SPECIAL AND PRETTY.

Butter Stacked Biscuits

2 1/2 cups plain flour
1 teaspoon baking powder
1 teaspoon baking soda
1 teaspoon salt
1 tablespoon sugar
4 tablespoons shortening
1 cup buttermilk, at room temperature
1/2 package yeast

- **Sift all dry ingredients together and cut in the shortening.**

- Dissolve the yeast in the buttermilk (room temperature).

- **Stir into flour mixture and roll out very thin, about 1/4 inch using a floured board.**

- Cut with biscuit cutter and butter the tops. Place one biscuit on top of another in buttery pairs.

- **Set in warm spot to rise, for almost an hour, before baking them in a 450° oven 10-12 minutes or until golden brown.**

FOR AN ADDED TREAT,

fry about 6 slices of bacon in an iron skillet until crisp.
Crumble and add it to the cornbread mixture before baking.
Pour almost all of the bacon grease out of the skillet

AND USE THAT PAN TO BAKE YOUR CORNBREAD.

Old-Fashioned CORN BREAD IN BLACK SKILLET

3 teaspoons bacon drippings
2 cups buttermilk
1 large egg
1 cup self-rising cornmeal
1 cup self-rising flour

- **Coat the bottom and sides of a 10" iron skillet with bacon drippings.**
- Preheat the oven to 450° and heat the skillet until piping hot.
- **Mix buttermilk and egg together.**
- Add cornmeal and flour; mix well.
- **Pour into piping hot skillet and bake 20-25 minutes until golden brown. Serve hot.**

MiMi's Knuckle Biscuits

2 cups self-rising flour (White Lily only)
1/2 teaspoon sugar
1/2 cup shortening, chilled
1 cup buttermilk
Add a pinch of baking soda

- Sift flour and sugar into mixing bowl.
- **Cut in shortening until mixture is coarse.**
- Add buttermilk and baking soda.
- **Lightly mix (do not over mix).**
- Turn dough onto a lightly floured surface and knead two or three times.
- **Roll out 1/2 inch thick. Cut dough with biscuit cutter, being careful not to twist the cutter.**
- Bake 450º 10-12 minutes or until golden brown. Brush with melted butter.

These **DELICIOUS** biscuits can be made up to 2 hours
ahead and wrapped in plastic wrap and refrigerated until ready to use.
Perfect to bake after you get home from church.
You may also pat this biscuit dough out into a square.
Then cut into square-shaped biscuits with a floured knife.

The kids love it when I make these because after they are baked,
you can see the imprint of my knuckles and fingers, and they think it's neat,
not to mention how **INCREDIBLY GOOD** they are.

Black-Eyed Pea Corn Bread

1 cup yellow or white corn meal
1/2 cup flour
1 teaspoon salt
1/2 teaspoon soda
2 eggs, slightly beaten
1 cup buttermilk
1/2 cup canola oil
1 onion, chopped
2 jalapeno peppers, chopped
3/4 cup cream-style corn
1 pound sausage
1 can black-eyed peas, drained
1/2 pound grated cheddar cheese

- **Brown sausage, stirring to crumble; drain. Mix together dry ingredients; add buttermilk, oil, eggs and corn.**
- Mix well and add other ingredients; mix.
- **Pour into a 9 x 13 lightly-oiled pan.**
- Bake at 400º for 40-50 minutes.

Grandma Ray's HUSH PUPPIES

1 cup plain cornmeal
1 cup self-rising flour
1/2 cup onion, finely chopped
1/2 baking potato, finely chopped
2 tablespoons sugar
1 1/2 cups milk
1 tablespoon chopped garlic
Dash of Louisiana hot sauce
2 eggs, beaten
shortening or vegetable oil for frying

- Mix dry ingredients together.
- **Add onion, potato, milk, garlic, eggs and hot sauce. Batter should be a little stiff.**
- Drop by spoonfuls into hot oil and fry to golden brown.

HUSH PUPPIES

THESE HUSH PUPPIES ARE BEST FRIED IN THE SAME GREASE THAT FISH HAVE BEEN FRIED IN.

Desserts

Our Desserts

"Made Fresh every day by my daughter Myra,"
she arrives early to the restaurant and surprises
everyone each day on what she has created.

Myra always fixes the basics:
Buttermilk Walnut Pie, Milk Cake,
Chocolate Delight and Chocolate Midnight Cake.
Definitely Ivy House Favorites.

She is available to do your
holiday baking, if needed.
She also creates that special birthday cake with her
handmade layered pound cake,
topped with a delightful buttercream icing.

Myra and Waica make a great team.
Myra bakes the cakes and Waica decorates
the specialty cakes
to create something
unique and original.

The Ivy House
Desserts

181

Milk Cake

1 box cake mix, yellow or white
2 (12-oz.) cans evaporated milk
1 can condensed milk
1 (12-oz.) carton Cool Whip
1 can flaked coconut, optional

- **Mix and bake cake as directed on package in a 9 x 13 pan.**
- When you remove from the oven, poke holes in warm cake.
- **Mix the two milks and pour over the warm cake.**
- Allow to cool in the refrigerator for at least 2-3 hours.
- **Spread the cool whip over top of cake and sprinkle coconut over top.**

THIS CAKE MAY BE GARNISHED WITH SLICED
STRAWBERRIES, BLUEBERRIES,
KIWI OR ANY OTHER OF YOUR FAVORITE FRUITS.

Lemon Chiffon Cake

1 box white cake mix
2 cups milk
2 tablespoons sour cream
1/2 cup oil
3 eggs
1-1/2 boxes lemon jello

- **Mix, pour, bake in 4 layer cake pans.**
- Bake at 325° until done to touch. (Don't over cook!)

FROSTING

1 box powdered sugar
1-8oz. package cream cheese
1-12oz. container cool whip
1 teaspoon vanilla

- Beat cream cheese until creamy and then add powdered sugar, cool whip, and vanilla. (Set aside and make Lemon Sauce.)

LEMON SAUCE

3 egg yolks
3/4 cup sugar
4 tablespoons butter
1/3 cup fresh lemon juice
1 tablespoon lemon zest

- **Mix yolks, sugar, and butter and stir constantly until thickened over medium heat and then add the lemon juice and zest, then cool.**
- Spread frosting over first layer and then pour 1/4 lemon sauce on. Continue with the 4 layers making sure you end with the lemon sauce on top.

TIPS:
Use lemons at room temperature because the cold ones cause lumps.
Grate lemon zest before cutting and juicing.

              Pictured on page 14

Chocolate Midnight Cake

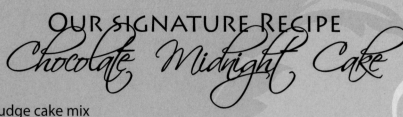

1 box chocolate fudge cake mix
1 cup sour cream
3 eggs
1/2 cup vegetable oil
1 2/3 cup milk

- **Combine cake mix, sour cream, eggs, milk and oil in mixture.**
- Blend well. Bake in three 9" cake pans for 20 minutes in a 325° oven.
- **Cool before icing.**

ICING

1 jar marshmallow cream
1 (8-oz.) carton whipped topping

- **Combine the marshmallow cream and whipped topping.**
- Ice the layers, assembling on a cake plate.
- **Optional Icing - Page 226. Rocky Road frosting.**

FUDGE SAUCE

2 cups granulated sugar
1/4 cup cocoa
1/4 teaspoon salt
1 (12-oz.) can evaporated milk
1 stick butter
1 teaspoon vanilla flavoring

- **Combine all ingredients, except the vanilla, in a heavy sauce pan and boil fast for 2 minutes, stirring constantly.**
- Remove from heat, add the vanilla, and beat until creamy.
- **Drizzle fudge sauce over top of the cake.**

WHEN SERVING THIS CAKE, DRIZZLE A LITTLE OF THE
WARM FUDGE SAUCE OVER EACH SLICE. ABSOLUTELY DIVINE!

Pictured on page 16

PaPa's Ole' Flat Cake WITH STRAWBERRIES

2 sticks butter, softened
2 cups sugar
3 cups self-rising flour
4 eggs
1 cup milk
1 teaspoon vanilla extract

- **In a large mixing bowl, beat butter and sugar until light and fluffy.**
- Add eggs, one at a time, beating well after each addition.
- **Sift flour, add to batter alternately with milk, beginning and ending with flour.**
- Add vanilla. Pour batter into cake pans that have been greased and dusted with flour.
- **Bake in 325° oven for 18-20 minutes until light brown.**
- Don't overcook. Allow to cool thoroughly.
- **Ice the layers and spoon thawed, frozen strawberries on each layer and top of cake.**

Cream Cheese Icing

1 stick butter, softened
2 (8-oz.) packages cream cheese, softened
2 (16-oz.) boxes confectioners sugar
2 teaspoons vanilla
1 cup chopped pecans

- **Mix all ingredients, except pecans, in a mixer until creamy and light.**
- Add chopped pecans and stir. Spread on three cake layers.

DESSERTS

Red Velvet Cake

1/2 cup butter
1 1/2 cups sugar
2 eggs
2 ounces red food coloring
2 tablespoons cocoa
2 1/4 cups cake flour, sifted
1 teaspoon salt
1 teaspoon soda
1 teaspoon vanilla
1 cup buttermilk
2 tablespoons vinegar

- **Cream together the Crisco and sugar and beat until fluffy.**
- Add eggs one at a time and blend well. Mix the flour, baking soda, salt and cocoa.
- **Mix the buttermilk, vinegar, food coloring, and vanilla.**
- Add flour and milk alternately to the creamed mixture, beginning and ending with the flour.
- **Blend well, but do not over beat.**
- Pour into 3 greased and floured 9" cake pans and bake at 350° for 18-20 minutes.
- **Cool and ice with cream cheese icing.**

RED VELVET CAKE

Cream Cheese Icing (FOR RED VELVET CAKE)

2 (8-oz.) packages cream cheese
1 stick butter
2 (16-oz.) boxes powdered sugar
2 teaspoons vanilla

- Melt butter and cream cheese together in microwave.

- **Beat all ingredients together until well blended and creamy.**

- Frost between layers, and on the top and sides of the cake.

ICING FOR

RED VELVET

My sweet friend Leslie Paramore gave me this recipe

AND WE HAVE JUST RELISHED IT.

She is such a dear friend to our family, both she and her husband Mike.
Leslie has also helped me countless hours gathering and organizing my recipes.

1-2-3-4 Cake

1 cup butter
2 cups sugar
3 cups self-rising flour
4 eggs
1 cup milk
1 teaspoon vanilla flavoring

- **In a mixer, beat butter and sugar until light and fluffy.**

- Add eggs one at a time, beating well after each addition.

- **Sift flour and add to the butter mixture alternately with the milk.**

- Add the vanilla and blend. Pour batter into three 9" cake pans, greased and floured.

- **Bake at 325° for 20 minutes or until sides of the cake begin to pull away from the pan.**

- Do not over bake. Ice cake with your favorite icing. (Chocolate fudge or cream cheese icing, garnished with roasted pecans are two of our favorites and always a hit with family and friends.)

Ooey Gooey Cake

1 yellow cake mix
1 stick butter, soft
3 eggs
1 box confectioners sugar
1 (8-oz.) package cream cheese

- **Mix the cake mix, butter and 1 egg in mixer until smooth and spreadable.**
- Pat in bottom of 9 x 13 baking pan.
- **Mix the sugar, cream cheese and remaining eggs (cream the cream cheese first, very well).**
- Pour over top of cake mixture.
- **Bake at 300° for approximately 25 minutes until golden brown.**
- Cool before serving.

OOEY GOOEY

FOR LEMON FLAVOR LOVERS,
JUST SUBSTITUTE A LEMON CAKE MIX IN PLACE OF THE YELLOW CAKE AND
YOU WILL HAVE A SPECIAL TREAT!
EVELYN HAS MADE THIS DESSERT SINCE SHE HAS BEEN 10 YEARS OLD.

Hummingbird Cake

3 cups self-rising flour
2 cups sugar
1 teaspoon cinnamon
3 eggs, lightly beaten
1 cup vegetable oil
1/2 cup buttermilk
1 1/2 teaspoons vanilla
1 (8-oz.) can crushed pineapple, undrained
1 cup chopped pecans
2 cups mashed ripe bananas, about 5-6 medium
1 cup coconut

- **Combine dry ingredients.**
- Add eggs, oil and buttermilk, stirring by hand until the dry ingredients are well moistened. Do not beat in a mixer. Stir in vanilla, pineapple, pecans, bananas and coconut.
- **Pour into 3 greased and floured 9" round cake pans.**
- Bake 25-35 minutes.
- **Cool and ice with cream cheese icing.**

Cream Cheese Icing

1 stick butter, softened
2 (8-oz.) packages cream cheese, softened
2 (16-oz.) boxes powdered sugar
2 teaspoons vanilla
1 cup chopped pecans

- **Mix all ingredients, except pecans, in a mixer until creamy and light.**
- Add chopped pecans and stir. Spread on three cake layers.

Coconut Dream Cake

1 box yellow cake mix
1/3 cup sour cream
3 eggs
1/2 cup vegetable oil
1 cup milk

- **Prepare cake mix, pour in 3 greased 9" pans, cool completly,**
- Bake at 350º **for 15-20 minutes**.
- **Chill.**

ICING

2 cups powdered sugar
1 (8-oz.) carton whipped topping
1 pint sour cream
1(12-oz.) package coconut

- Combine sugar, whipped topping, sour cream and coconut.
- **Chill.**
- Spread between layers, top and sides of cake. Seal cake in an airtight container.
- **Refrigerate for three days before serving, or if you can't stand it eat the next day.**

COCONUT DREAM CAKE

Layered Cheese Cake

2 (8-oz.) packages cream cheese
2 cans condensed milk
6 eggs
1/4 teaspoon salt
1/2 cup lemon juice, fresh squeezed
1 large carton whipped topping
2 1/2 cups graham cracker crumbs
6 tablespoons butter, slightly melted

- **Combine the graham cracker crumbs and melted butter, blending until well moistened.**
- Pat crumbs into bottom of a 9 x 13 baking pan.
- **Mix cream cheese and condensed milk.**
- Add eggs and beat, then add the 1/2 cup lemon juice and salt.
- **Pour into crust and bake at 325° for 30 minutes.**
- Remove from oven and cool.
- **Cut cheesecake into half while still in the pan.**
- Remove one half and place on a flat plate.
- **Spread with whipped topping.**
- Stack remaining half on top of the layer and ice top and sides with remaining topping, just like a regular cake.
- **Garnish with fresh fruit, berries, or flowers.**

LAYERED CHEESE CAKE

22-minute Cake & Icing

2 cups plain flour
2 cups sugar
3 tablespoons cocoa
1 stick butter or margarine
1 cup water
1/2 cup buttermilk
1 teaspoon soda
2 eggs
1 teaspoon cinnamon
1 teaspoon vanilla

- **Sift together the flour, sugar, salt, soda and cinnamon; set aside.**
- In a pot, put butter, water, and cocoa and bring to a boil slowly. When boiled and dissolved, pour into the sifted flour mixture.
- **Stir until blended, then add buttermilk and eggs.**
- Mix well and add vanilla. Pour into a greased and floured sheet pan (11 x 15) and bake for 20 minutes at 400º.

ICING

1 stick butter or margarine
4 tablespoons cocoa
6 tablespoons milk
1 (16-oz.) powdered sugar
1 teaspoon vanilla
1 cup chopped pecans, optional

- **In a sauce pan combine butter, milk and cocoa.**
- Mix and cook over medium heat.
- **Heat until boilng; remove from heat**
- Add powdered sugar, vanilla and mix.
- **Pour over Hot cake**

OUR SWEET PRECIOUS MS. RUBY WISE BROUGHT THIS TO WORK ONE DAY.
I HAVE LOVED AND SERVED THIS CAKE EVER SINCE.

German Chocolate Layered Cake

2 cups all-purpose cake flour, unsifted
1 1/2 cups sugar
1 teaspoon baking soda
1/2 teaspoon baking powder
1/2 teaspoon salt
2/3 cup butter or margarine
1 cup buttermilk
1 teaspoon vanilla
2 eggs
1 (4-oz.) package German's Sweet Chocolate, melted

- **In a large mixing bowl, on low speed, soften butter.**
- Stir together the flour, sugar, soda, baking powder and salt.
- **Add to the butter, buttermilk, vanilla, eggs and melted chocolate; blend well.**
- Beat 3 minutes at medium speed, scraping bowl frequently.
- **Pour into 2 well-greased and floured 9" cake pans.**
- Bake at 350º for about 35 minutes, or until cake tests done.
- **Cool in pans 15 minutes; then remove from pans.**
- Finish cooling on rack.
- **Spread the coconut pecan frosting between layers and over top.**

Coconut-Pecan Frosting on next page

Coconut-Pecan Frosting

1 cup canned cream (evaporated milk)
1 cup sugar
3 egg yolks, slightly beaten
1 stick butter or margarine
1 teaspoon vanilla
11/3 cups coconut
1 cup pecans, chopped

- **Combine milk, sugar, egg yolks, butter and vanilla in sauce pan.**
- Cook over medium heat, stirring constantly, until mixture thickens.
- **Remove from heat. Add coconut and pecans.**
- Beat until of spreading consistency.
- **Put between layers and on top of cake.**

Pecan Pound Cake

2 sticks butter
2 cups sugar
6 eggs
2 cups plain flour
1/2 cup sour cream
1 teaspoon vanilla
2 cups chopped pecans
1/2 cup sour cream
1 pinch of salt

- **Cream together butter and sugar. Add eggs one at a time until just blended. Add 1 cup flour and salt, blend. Add sour cream, blend. Add 1 cup flour, blend.**
- Add vanilla and fold in pecans, pour into a greased tube pan. Bake in 325^0 oven for 1 hour or until done.

Candy Cake

1 cup butter
2 cups sugar
4 eggs, well beaten
1 teaspoon soda
1/2 cup buttermilk
3 1/2 cups plain flour, sifted
1 can Angel Flake Coconut
1(12-oz.) box of dates
1 (16-oz.) bag orange slice candy, chopped
2 cups chopped pecans

- **Cream butter, sugar, and eggs in mixer.**
- Mix soda in buttermilk. (Use a 1-cup measure because it will swell over the top).
- **Alternately add milk and 3 cups of the flour to the creamed mixture.**
- Mix well and add coconut. Combine the remaining 1/4 cup of flour with chopped dates, orange slices and pecans.
- Bake at 275°- 300° for 2 1/2 hours. In bunt cake pan.
- **Pour glaze over cake while hot.**

glaze

MIX 1 CUP ORANGE JUICE WITH 2 CUPS POWDERED
SUGAR AND POUR OVER HOT CAKE,
ALLOWING IT TO RUN DOWN SIDES, UNDER AND OVER,
USING EVERY BIT. LEAVE OVERNIGHT IN PAN.

Pineapple Pound Cake

3 cups granulated sugar
2 cups shortening
9 eggs
3 cups flour
1/2 teaspoon salt
1/2 teaspoon vanilla
1 (16-oz.) can crushed pineapple
1/2 box powdered sugar

- **Cream the granulated sugar and shortening. Sift the flour, salt and baking powder together and set aside.**
- Add eggs and flour mixture to sugar and shortening alternately.
- **Add 3 eggs for every cup of flour mixture until all are used. Add vanilla.**
- Drain the pineapple, reserving the juice. Add the pineapple to the mixture.
- **Grease and flour a large tube pan.**
- Pour the batter into the pan and bake at 300° for 1 hour.
- **Make a glaze from pineapple juice and powdered sugar.**
- Pour over warm cake.

"MY SISTER NETTIE'S FAVORITE CAKE."
I MADE THIS FOR HER ON HER BIRTHDAY, EVERY YEAR.

Cheesecake

1 cup all purpose flour
1/2 cup sugar
1/2 cup butter softened
1 egg yolk
1 tablespoon grated lemon peel
5 pks cream cheese (8 ounces each)
1 3/4 cups sugar
3 tablespoons flour

1/4 teaspoon salt
1 tablespoon grated orange peel
1 tablespoon grated lemon peel
5 eggs
2 yolks
1/4 cup whipping cream
1/3 cup toasted silvered almonds

- **Heat oven 400°, grease 9 - inch spring form pan lightly, remove bottom.**
- Mix 1 cup flour, 1/4 cup sugar, the butter, 1 yolk and 1 tablespoon lemon peel with hands.
- **Press 1/3 of mixture evenly on bottom of pan: place on baking sheet.**
- Bake until golden brown, 8-10 minutes: cool.
- **Assemble bottom and side of pan, secure side. Press remaining mixture all the way up the side of the pan.**
- Heat oven to 475°.
- **Beat cream cheese, 1 3/4 cups sugar, 3 tablespoons flour, the salt, orange peel, lemon peel and 2 of the eggs in large mixer bowl until smooth.**
- Continue beating, adding remaining eggs and 2 egg yolks, 1 at a time.

- **Beat in 1/4 cup whipping cream on low speed. Pour into pan.**
- Bake 15 min.reduce oven temperature to 200°.
- **Bake 1 hour. Turn off oven. Leave cheesecake 15 minutes.**
- Cool 1/2 hour. Refrigerate at least 12 hours.
- **Loosen cheesecake from side of pan.**
- Beat 3/4 cup whipping cream in chilled bowl until stiff.
- **Spread whipped cream over top of cheesecake and decorate with almonds.**
- 20 to 22 servings.

CHEESECAKE

My sweet Diane Pierce loves cheesecake. She makes extra special ones all the time and shares them with us. Diane is a very special person to me,

TRULY ONE OF MY GIRLS.

DESSERTS

White Chocolate Cake

1/3 pound white chocolate
1/2 cup water
1 cup butter, softened
2 cups sugar, divided
4 eggs, separated
1 teaspoon vanilla

3 cups plain flour
1 1/2 teaspoon baking powder
1/2 teaspoon salt
1 cup buttermilk
1 cup chopped nuts
1 (7-oz.) package flaked coconut

- **Melt chocolate and water and allow to cool.**
- Cream butter and 1 1/2 cups sugar until light and fluffy.
- **Add egg yolks, one at a time, beating well after each addition.**
- Stir in vanilla. Sift flour, baking powder and salt together.
- **Combine dry ingredients, chocolate mixture, creamed mixture and buttermilk.**
- Stir in nuts and coconut. Beat egg whites until peaks form; fold into batter.
- **Spread into 3 greased and floured 9" round cake pans and bake at 350° for 30-35 minutes. Cool before frosting.**

Frosting

1 (8-oz.) package cream cheese, softened
1/2 cup butter
1 (16-oz.) box powdered sugar
Few drops of evaporated milk
1 teaspoon vanilla

- **Cream butter and cream cheese until fluffy and smooth.**
- Gradually add powdered sugar, add vanilla. (Add a few drops of canned cream, if needed, to bring to spreading consistency.)
- **Spread between layers and on top and sides of cake.**

For the Sour Cream Pound Cake you can also add any of your favorite extracts, i.e., lemon, orange, almond, pineapple, etc. Along with the vanilla.

IT WILL GIVE IT YOUR SPECIAL TASTE.

Sour Cream Pound Cake

2 3/4 cups sugar
1 cup butter
6 eggs
3 cups all-purpose flour, sifted
1/2 teaspoon salt, optional
1/4 teaspoon baking soda
1 cup sour cream
1 teaspoon vanilla extract

- **In a mixer, cream together sugar and butter until light and fluffy.**

- Add eggs one at a time, beating well after each addition.

- **Sift together flour, salt and soda. Add to creamed mixture alternately with sour cream, beating after each addition.**

- Add vanilla and beat well. Pour into greased and lightly floured 10" tube pan and bake at 300° for 1 1/2 hours or until cake tests done.

- **Cool 15 minutes and remove from pan. When cool, sprinkle with powered sugar, if desired.**

PUMPKIN PIE

Pumpkin Pie

1 (15-oz.) package refrigerated pie crusts
3/4 cup sugar
1 1/2 teaspoons pumpkin pie spice
1/2 teaspoon salt
1(16-oz.) can pumpkin
1 (12-oz.) can evaporated milk
2 eggs, beaten

- **In a large bowl, combine all filling ingredients; blend well.**
- Place pie crust into a 9" pie pan and pour filling into it.
- **Bake in a preheated oven at 325° 25-30 minutes or until a knife blade stuck in the center comes out clean.**
- Cool and top with whipped topping.

Pumpkin Roll

3 eggs, beaten
1 cup sugar
1 teaspoon baking soda
3/4 cup flour
2/3 cup pumpkin
1/2 teaspoon cinnamon
1/2 cup chopped walnuts or pecans

- **Line jelly roll pan or cookie sheet with wax paper, and grease or spray well.**
- Mix in bowl one ingredient at a time with wire whisk. Pour evenly into pan and sprinkle with chopped nuts. Bake at 375° for 15 minutes.
- **While cake is in oven, place a linen dish towel on table and sprinkle generously with powdered sugar.**
- Take cake out and immediately turn out on dish towel, nuts side down.
- **Then peel off wax paper. Roll cake with the towel and let stand rolled for approximately 2 hours until cool.**
- Then unroll the cake and spread filling evenly, then roll the cake back up and slice to serve.

FILLING

1 stick butter, softened
2 (8 oz.) packages cream cheese, softened
2 (16 oz.) boxes powered sugar
3 teaspoons of vanilla
1 small carton whipped topping

- **Cream butter, cream cheese and powered sugar.**
- Add vanilla.
- **Add whipped topping and mix well.**

Banana Split Cake

2 cups graham cracker crumbs
1/2 cup melted butter
2 cups powdered sugar
2 eggs
1 cup butter, softened
6 bananas, peeled and halved lengthwise

1 (20 oz.) can crushed pineapple, drained
1 quart fresh strawberries halved
1 (16 oz.) package frozen whipped topping,
   thawed container
1 cup chopped walnuts toasted

- **Combine cracker crumbs and melted butter thoroughly and press into bottom of 9x13 dish. Chill in freezer for at least 15 minutes.**

- Beat powdered sugar, eggs and softened butter at medium speed for 20 minutes. (This step is important, so don't try to save time.)

- **Spread the creamy mixture over the cracker crumbs, then top with banana halves**

- Combine crushed pineapple, fresh strawberries and walnuts and fold into whipped topping.

- **Spread over bananas.**

- Chill until ready to serve.

BANANA SPLIT CAKE
In Memory of

Michael Lester Micheletti

March 3, 1952 - May 12, 1977

This Banana Split Cake was Michael Sr.'s (Waica and Michael's Daddy) very favorite, he wished for it almost every Sunday. I was hesitant to make it because I was so busy Sunday morning trying to get lunch started before we left for church. Hand mixing for 20 minutes was too long. So he would come over and get everything ready for me to assemble the cake. We had a special time together making this dessert. After he passed away in 1977, I haven't made this recipe and I probably won't, but it sure is good and I wanted to share this special dessert with you.

"A SPECIAL DESSERT FOR A SPECIAL MAN!"

Buttermilk Walnut Pie

1 stick butter
1 1/2 cups sugar
2 teaspoons vanilla
3 eggs
3 tablespoons plain flour
1 pinch salt
1 cup buttermilk
1 cup walnuts, chopped
1 9" pie crust

- **Cream butter, sugar and vanilla.**
- Add eggs, flour and salt. Beat well.
- Fold in buttermilk and pour mixture into crust.
- **Sprinkle 1 cup chopped walnuts on bottom of crust.**
- **Bake at 300° 1 1/2 hours or until middle is set.**

AN IVY HOUSE FAVORITE

Egg Custard Pie

1 9" unbaked pie crust
3 eggs, beaten
3/4 cup white sugar
1/4 teaspoon salt
1 teaspoon vanilla
1 egg white
2 1/2 cups scalded milk
1/4 teaspoon ground nutmeg
3 drops yellow food coloring, optional

- **Mix together eggs, sugar, salt and vanilla.**
- Stir well.
- **Blend in the scalded milk.**
- For a more yellow color, add a few drops of yellow food coloring.
- **Place pie crust in pan and brush inside bottom and sides of shell with egg white to help prevent a soggy crust.**
- Pour custard mixture into pie crust. Sprinkle with nutmeg.
- **Bake in a preheated 350° oven 30-35 minutes or until a knife inserted near center comes out clean.**
- Cool on rack.

Cream Pie

1/3 cup plain flour, sifted (or 1/4 cup cornstarch)
3/4 cup sugar
1/4 teaspoon salt
2 cups milk, scalded
3 egg yolks, slightly beaten
2 tablespoons butter
1/2 teaspoon vanilla
1 baked 9" pastry shell

CREAM PIE

- **Mix flour, sugar and salt.**
- Gradually add milk and cook over medium heat, stirring until mixture thickens and boils. Cook 2 minutes more.
- **Remove from heat and add small amount of mixture to egg yolks.**
- Add yolks to hot mixture. Cook until thick, stirring constantly.
- **Add butter and vanilla. Cool slightly.**
- Pour into baked pastry shell and allow to cool a little longer.
- **Cover with meringue and bake at 350° 12-15 minutes.**

THERE ARE SO MANY DIFFERENT PIES YOU CAN CREATE USING THIS BASIC RECIPE.

Banana: Slice 3 bananas into shell before adding filling.

Butterscotch: Substitute 1 cup brown sugar for 2/3 cup sugar and increase butter to 3 tablespoons.

Chocolate: Sift 1/4 cup cocoa, or to taste.

MERINGUE

Perfect Meringue FOR CREAM PIES

3 egg whites, at room temperature
1/4 teaspoon salt
1/4 teaspoon cornstarch
6 tablespoons sugar
1/2 teaspoon vanilla
1/8 teaspoon cream of tartar

- **Beat egg whites and salt until frothy.**
- Add cornstarch and cream of tartar.
- **Add sugar, one tablespoon at a time.**
- Beat until stiff and glossy and tip holds a point.
- **Add vanilla. Swirl meringue onto pie; seal to edges of crust.**
- Bake at 350° for 12-15 minutes.

Pecan Pie

3/4 cup white sugar (or 1 cup light or dark brown)
3/4 cup white corn syrup
2 tablespoons milk
1 tablespoon plain flour
2 tablespoons butter, melted
3-4 eggs, slightly beaten
1 teaspoon vanilla
1 cup pecans chopped
1 cup pecan halves
1 9" pie crust, unbaked

- **Combine all ingredients, except the pecan halves.**
- Mix and stir well by hand. Pour into unbaked pie shell.
- **Place pecan halves on top and bake in a preheated 325° oven 40-45 minutes or until well set.**

PECAN PIE

Fudge Pie

1 1/2 cup sugar
1/2 cup melted butter
3 1/2 tbsp. cocoa
2 Eggs
1 tsp. vanilla
1 5oz. canned cream (evaporated milk)
1-9" unbaked pie shell

- **Beat eggs slightly and add melted butter, mixing well.**
- Add remaining ingredients and blend.
- **Pour into unbaked pie shell and bake at 325° for 25-30 minutes.**

Baked Pumpkin Crunch Cake

1 (16-oz.) can pumpkin
3 tablespoons pumpkin pie spice
3 eggs
1 butter recipe cake mix (I use Duncan Hines)
1 1/2 sticks butter, melted
1 cup milk
1 cup chopped pecans

- **Mix pumpkin, pie spice and eggs.**
- Pour into sprayed 9 x 13 baking dish.
- **Sprinkle cake mix over pumpkin.**
- Mix melted butter and nuts and pour over cake mix.
- **Bake at 325° for 45 minutes until golden brown.**

Carrot Cake WITH CREAM CHEESE ICING

CARROT CAKE

2 cups sugar
1 1/2 cups vegetable oil
4 eggs
2 cups plain flour
1 teaspoon salt
2 teaspoons soda
3 teaspoons cinnamon
3 cups carrots, finely grated

DESSERT

- **Mix the sugar, oil and eggs well.**
- Combine the flour, salt, soda and cinnamon and add to the egg mixture, blending well.
- **Add the grated carrots.**
- Let batter stand 30 minutes.
- **Pour into 3 greased and floured cake pans and bake at 325° for 30 minutes.**
- Cool completely and frost with cream cheese icing.

1 box powered sugar
1 - 8 oz. package of cream cheese
1/2 stick butter or margarine
1 teaspoon vanilla

- **Cream butter and cream cheese.**
- Add powdered sugar.
- **Add vanilla**

This is my sweet Leslie Paramore's recipe.
After eating it I told her I just had to have it for the cookbook.

Miniature Cheesecake Pies

3 (8-oz.) packages cream cheese
1 cup sugar
4 eggs
1 1/2 teaspoons vanilla
Vanilla wafer cookies

- **Cream the sugar and the cream cheese.**
- Add eggs one at a time, beating after each addition.
- **Add vanilla.**
- **Place one cookie in bottom of muffin paper**
- Spoon into miniature, paper-lined muffin tins.
- **Bake at 300° for 25 minutes. Remove from oven and add topping (see below).**

Topping

2 cups sour cream
1/2 cup sugar
1 teaspoon vanilla

- **Mix all ingredients and spoon over top of miniature pies.**
- Bake another 10 minutes.

THESE ARE PERFECT FOR YOUR

PARTIES, SHOWERS, AND RECEPTIONS.

Chocolate Delight

FIRST LAYER

1 1/2 cups plain flour
1 1/2 sticks butter
1 1/2 cup nuts, finely chopped

- **Mix all ingredients in a mixer and press into bottom of a 9 x 13 baking dish and bake in a 350° oven for 20 minutes or until lightly browned.**
- Completely cool.

SECOND LAYER

1 cup confectioners sugar

1 (8-oz.) package cream cheese, room temperature

1 (8-oz.) carton whipped topping

- **Combine all ingredients in a mixer and mix well.**
- Spread over cooled crust.

DELIGHT

Chocolate Delight — LAYERS 3-4

THIRD LAYER

2 small boxes instant chocolate pudding
3 cups milk

- **In a mixer, combine the pudding mix and milk and whisk until smooth.**
- Spread over the cream cheese layer.

FOURTH LAYER

1 large carton whipped topping

- **Spread over pudding layer.**
- Refrigerate until cold.

MiMi's Bread Puddin'

3 eggs
3 cups milk
6 slices day-old white bread, cut into 1/2" pieces
1 stick butter, softened
1 cup sugar
1/8 teaspoon salt
1 teaspoon vanilla
1 teaspoon cinnamon
1/4 cup sliced almonds, optional

DESSERT

- **Butter the bread and cut into 1/2 pieces.**
- Place in a sprayed 9 x 13 baking dish.
- **In a bowl beat eggs well, one at a time.**
- Add milk, vanilla, sugar and salt, blend by hand.
- **Pour milk mixture over top of bread and let soak for 30 minutes.**
- Sprinkle almonds over top.
- **Place the pudding in a preheated 325° oven and place a pan of water on the rack beneath the baking dish. Bake for 1 1/4 hours.**
- Serve in dessert dishes and top with custard (optional).

For variety, raisins, pineapple, blackberries, blueberries, or peaches could
be added to the pudding prior to baking.
At the Ivy House, I always make soft custard to serve over ours,
AND OUR GUESTS HAVE GIVEN IT RAVING REVIEWS.

CUSTARD ON NEXT PAGE

Custard for Bread Puddin'

2 cups milk
4 egg yolks
1/2 cup sugar
1/4 teaspoon salt
3 tablespoons cornstarch
2 tablespoons butter
1 teaspoon vanilla

- **In a sauce pan, lightly beat the egg yolks and add about a cup of the milk, stirring to blend.**

- Add sugar, salt and cornstarch and mix well.

- **Add remaining milk. Cook over medium heat, stirring constantly until thickened.**

- Remove from heat and add the butter and vanilla. Spoon over bread pudding as it is served.

Blueberry or Cherry Torte

1 box butter cake mix
6 eggs
2/3 cup water
1 stick butter, softened
1 box instant vanilla pudding

- **Mix well and pour into 4 greased and floured round cake pans.**
- Bake at 325º degrees until done to touch (don't overcook).

FROSTING

1 box powdered sugar
1-8oz. package cream cheese (Room temperature)
1-12oz. container cool whip
1 teaspoon vanilla

FILLING

1 can blueberry or cherry pie filling

- **Beat cream cheese until creamy and then add powdered sugar, cool whip, and vanilla.**
- Spread frosting over first layer and then pour on 1/4 of the pie filling.
- **Continue with each layer, making sure you end with the pie filling on top. Pretty! Pretty!**

BLUEBERRY TORTE FEATURED ON THE COVER

Apple Dumplings

2 pie crusts, unbaked
8 tablespoons sugar
1 teaspoon cinnamon
1/2 teaspoon butter
1 cup water
1/2 cup brown sugar
1/4 cup butter, melted
8 apples

- **Roll pie crusts as thin as possible, making squares.**
- Cut each crust into 4 pieces. Cut out holes in top of apples and remove seeds.
- **Place each apple on a square of pastry.**
- Mix the 8 tablespoons sugar, cinnamon and butter in small bowl.
- **Put approximately 1 tablespoon of the mixture in each apple.**
- Pull corners of square pastry together above apple and pinch together.
- **Place in a 9 x 13 baking dish.**
- Combine the water, brown sugar and 1/4 cup melted butter and pour over apples.
- **Bake at 425° for 35-45 minutes.**

Puff Pastry

2 tablespoons butter
1/4 cup boiling water
1/4 cup all-purpose flour
1/8 teaspoon salt
1 egg

- **Melt butter in boiling water.**
- Add flour and salt, stirring vigorously until mixture forms a ball.
- **Remove from heat and cool slightly.**
- Add egg and beat until smooth.
- Drop level teaspoonfuls of dough onto greased baking sheet.
- **Bake at 400° for 20 minutes.**
- Cool.
- **Cut a small hole into top of each puff pastry and fill with your favorite custard, cheese or vegetable.**

THESE PUFF PASTRIES ARE SO VERSATILE
THAT YOU CAN USE THEM FOR ANY PARTY OR SPECIAL OCCASION.

IN ADDITION TO MAKING DAINTY DESSERT TREATS,
they are perfect to use for many types of appetizers. Simply make a batch of your favorite filling – chicken salad, shrimp or crab salad, tuna salad, etc., and fill the pastries.

CRÈME

Crème Topping

TOPPING FOR FRUITS,
CUSTARDS AND BREAD PUDDING

YIELD: 1 1/4 cups

1/2 cup whipping cream
2 1/2 tablespoons powdered sugar
2 tablespoons sour cream
1/4 teaspoon vanilla extract

- **Combine all ingredients in a small mixing bowl.**

- Beat at high speed until soft peak forms.

Key Lime Pie

1 pie crust, baked
4 egg yolks
1 can condensed milk
2/3 cup key lime juice

- **Separate eggs, reserving the whites.**
- Use wire whisk and beat egg yolks.
- **Fold in condensed milk; add lime juice.**
- Mix well and pour into baked crust.
- **Top with meringue and bake until browned.**

Meringue

4 egg whites
1/4 teaspoon salt
1/2 cup sugar
1/2 teaspoon vanilla
1 teaspoon cornstarch
1/2 teaspoon cream of tartar

- **Beat egg whites, salt, cornstarch and cream of tartar until frothy. Gradually add the sugar and beat until glossy.**
- Add vanilla and continue beating until stiff peak forms. Swirl meringue on pie and bake at 325° for 12-15 minutes or lightly browned.

ICE CREAM

Ice Cream Cookie

2 cups Oreo cookies, crushed
1/4 cup butter, melted
1 (5 oz.) can evaporated milk
2 tablespoons butter
1/2 cup sugar
2 (1 oz.) blocks sweet chocolate squares
1/2 teaspoon vanilla
1 (8 oz.) carton whipped topping
1 quart vanilla ice cream
Chocolate shavings

- **Mix cookies and butter in a 9 x 13 baking, press down.**
- Soften the ice cream and spread on top of cookie mixture.
- **Return to freezer. In a saucepan, on medium heat, cook milk, butter, sugar, chocolate and vanilla until thickened.**
- Cool and spread on top of the ice cream.
- **Cover with whipped cream topping and sprinkle chocolate shavings on top.**
- Keep in freezer until ready to serve.

Surprise Banana Puddin'

1 large vanilla pudding (to cook)
1 large chocolate pudding (to cook)
1 medium carton whipped topping
1 large box vanilla wafers
4 bananas

- **Cook puddings separately as directed on the package.**
- Let cool. Fold in 1/2 the whipped topping in each cooked pudding.
- **In a large flat bottom glass bowl or serving dish, layer 1/2 the box of vanilla wafers; then layer 2 sliced bananas; then the chocolate pudding. Layer the remaining box of wafers, followed by 2 sliced bananas; then layer the vanilla pudding.**
- Crush several wafers to sprinkle on top.

YUMMY!

Grandma Ray's PEACH COBBLER

1-14 1/2 to 16 oz can sliced peaches, undrained
1 stick of butter
1 cup of self-rising flour
1 cup sugar
1 cup milk
1 teaspoon vanilla

- **Melt butter in a 9" x 13" baking dish.**
- Combine flour, sugar, vanilla and milk. Blend well and pour over melted butter.
- **Gently distribute peaches into batter and then drizzle the juice over the entire pan.**
- Bake at 350° for 35-40 minutes until golden brown.

COBBLER

I LIKE TO USE O'SAGE CANNED PEACHES IN THIS COBBLER, BUT ANY SLICED PEACHES WILL DO. IF YOU WANT MORE PEACHES DRAIN THE SECOND CAN, SO YOU ONLY USE THE JUICE OF ONE.

Rocky Road Frosting

1 (16 oz.) package semi-sweet chocolate morsels
1/4 cup butter
2 1/2 cups confectioners sugar, sifted
3 tablespoons scalded milk
1 teaspoon vanilla
1 egg
1 1/2 cup miniature marshmallows
1 cup toasted walnuts, chopped

- **Melt chocolate over hot boiling water.**
- Mix butter with sugar, milk and vanilla.
- **Beat in egg.**
- Add chocolate, stirring until morsels are melted and well blended.
- **Stir in marshmallows and walnuts.**

I THINK THIS ICING WOULD BE GREAT ON THE
MIDNIGHT CHOCOLATE CAKE
THAT WE SERVE AT THE IVY HOUSE.

Peach Bread Puddin'

1 (8-oz.) package cream cheese
2/3 cup sugar
4 eggs
1 cup milk
1/2 teaspoon almond flavoring
1 teaspoon lemon peel
1 teaspoon vanilla
3 1/2 cups dry bread cubes
1 (29-oz.) can peach halves
3 tablespoon raspberry jam
4 teaspoons sugar
1 1/4 teaspoon cinnamon
1/4 cup sliced almonds

- **Place the bread cubes in a 2 1/2 quart baking dish.**
- Beat the cream cheese and sugar together. Add eggs and beat well.
- **Add the milk, flavorings and lemon peel.**
- Pour mixture over the bread and allow to soak for approximately 30 minutes.
- **Drain the peaches and press the peach halves down into the pudding, just to the tops.**
- Mix the raspberry jam, 4 teaspoons cinnamon.
- **Spoon 1 1/2 -2 teaspoons of jam into center of each peach.**
- Sprinkle almonds over top.
- **Bake in a preheated 325° oven for 1 1/4 - 1 1/2 hours.**

TO MAKE YOUR FAVORITE
Colored Sugar

- **Put one to three drops of food coloring into a small jar.**
- Swirl the jar to coat the sides.
- **Add 1/4 to 1/3 cup granulated sugar and shake vigorously until sugar is evenly coated.**

"OF COURSE I MAKE MOSTLY PURPLE"
1-2 drops of red food coloring and 1-2 drops of blue food coloring

Chocolate Fudge Icing

2 cups white sugar
1/4 cup cocoa
1/4 teaspoon salt
2/3 cup canned cream (evaporated milk)
1 stick butter
1tsp. vanilla

- **Combine all ingredients in a heavy saucepan.**
- Boil fast for 2 minutes, stirring constantly.
- **Remove from heat and add vanilla.**
- Beat until cool and creamy and of spreading consistency.

TO USE AS A HOT FUDGE SAUCE INSTEAD OF ICING,
INCREASE MILK TO ONE FULL CAN (12 OZ.)

Chocolate's Butter Icing

2 (16 oz.) boxes powdered sugar
2 sticks butter, softened
1/2 cup cocoa
1 1/2 teaspoons vanilla
Pinch of salt, optional if using salted butter
Small amount of canned cream (evaporated milk)

- **In a large mixing bowl, combine sugar, butter and salt.**
- Mix on low speed of electric mixer until blended.
- **Add vanilla and beat on high.**
- Gradually add just enough milk to make icing creamy and of spreading consistency.

Old-Fashioned Lemon Cheese Icing

2 cups sugar
1 1/2 cups water
2 eggs
1/2 cup lemon juice
4 tablespoons cornstarch
2 tablespoons flour
1 1/2 sticks butter
1 teaspoon grated lemon rind
1/2 teaspoon salt

- **In a heavy saucepan, mix sugar, cornstarch, flour and salt; beat and add eggs; add water and mix well.**
- Add butter and lemon juice.
- **Cook over high heat, stirring constantly, until mixture begins to thicken.**
- Lower heat and continue to cook approximately 10 minutes more.
- **Mix will be very transparent.**
- Add rind.
- **Cool and spread on cake.**

Dribble Sweet Glaze

1 cup confectioners sugar
1 tablespoon milk
1/2 teaspoon vanilla

MIX ALL INGREDIENTS UNTIL WELL BLENDED AND SUGAR IS MELTED.

White Chocolate Buttercream Icing

2 (8 oz.) packages cream cheese (room temperature)
12 ounces white chocolate chips, melted
1 stick unsalted butter, softened
2 tablespoons fresh lemon juice

- **Beat cream cheese until smooth.**
- Gradually add melted white chocolate and blend well.
- **Beat in butter and lemon juice.**
- Continue beating until totally smooth before frosting cake.

WHITE CHOCOLATE

Crème Cheese Mints

YIELD: 8 Dozen

1 (8 oz.) package cream cheese
1/4 cup butter, softened
2 (16 oz.) boxes powdered sugar
1/2 teaspoon peppermint flavoring
6 drops red food coloring, optional

- **Combine in a saucepan the cream cheese and butter; cook over low heat until smooth.**

- Gradually stir in sugar.

- **Add food coloring, if desired.**

- Shape into 1" balls. Dip a 2" round cookie stamp, or bottom of glass into powdered sugar; press to flatten ball.

- **Place in single layer on cookie sheets and freeze, uncovered, for 4 hours or until firm.**

- Pack into layers of wax paper inside an airtight container and freeze.

MINTS

Lily Cookies

YIELDS 2-2 1/2 dozen cookies

1 cup butter
4 1/2 ounces cream cheese, room temperature
2 cups plain flour, sifted
2 heaping tablespoons of powdered sugar
3 tablespoons orange marmalade
Egg wash
Powdered sugar to garnish

- **Cream butter and cream cheese.**
- Add flour, sugar and chill for 1 hour.
- **Roll dough to 1/8 " thickness and cut with a 2" round cutter.**
- Flatten out the top portion slightly to resemble a lily.
- **Fold edges over, sealing well with egg wash.**
- Fill open end with 1/4 teaspoon marmalade.
- **Bake at 375° for 15 minutes.**
- Cool before dusting with powdered sugar.

LILY COOKIES

CRUST FOR
COBBLERS

Crust for Cobblers OR POT PIES

1 1/2 cups self-rising flour
1/2 cup Crisco shortening
1/3 cup milk

- **Cut shortening into flour with pastry blender or fork until fine crumbs form.**
- Add the milk, and stir until dough forms and pulls away from the side of the bowl.
- **Turn dough onto a floured board and kneed until smooth.**
- Roll dough in a rectangle and cut in strips.
- **Place over cobbler or pot pies and bake at 400° until brown.**

Grilled Peanut Butter & Jelly Sandwich

YIELD: One sandwich

2 slices bread
2 tablespoons peanut butter
2 tablespoons favorite jelly or jam
2 pats butter, softened

- **Put peanut butter on 1 slice of bread and jelly or jam on the other slice; put together.**
- Spread softened butter on both sides of the sandwich.
- **Toast in a skillet until golden brown.**

Chocolate Pudding

2 tbsp. flour
2 tbsp. cornstarch
1/2 tsp. salt
2/3 cup sugar
2 cups milk

3 egg yolks
1 tsp. vanilla
1 tbsp. butter
2 1/2 tbls. cocoa

- **Combine all ingredients together in a sauce pan.**
- **Cook over medium heat, stirring constantly, until thickened.**

THIS IS MY GRANDAUGHTER ALESHA'S FAVORITE.
SHE LOVES ANYTHING CHOCOLATE! QUICK AND TASTY!

Expressions FROM MiMi

My home is a treasure chest
In which I collect memories of my
family and friends.

The secret ingredient I add to all
our recipes is LOVE.

There is nothing like the aroma of
HOME - COOKING to bring your customers,
loved ones and family together.

Do not be overly concerned with the
interior of your home, its the inside
of your heart that people
will remember.

MIMI'S FAMOUS
Excuses for Eating

It's Sunday .... Honey, you don't diet on Sunday!

It's Friday .... GOOD DAY FOR DESSERT!

It's the WEEKEND! We don't diet on the weekends.

Sugar, you can eat whatever you want, just a little bit of it.

It's your birthday! You get to splurge on your birthday.

HONEY, I'VE GOT PLENTY ON THE STOVE.
NOW GET UP AND GET YOU ANOTHER PLATE.

"Food for the Soul"

WHEN DIFFICULT TIMES COME YOUR WAY REMEMBER THERE ARE PRECIOUS VERSES AND OUR SPECIAL PRAYER WARRIORS THAT KEEPS US LIFTED UP.

Praise the Lord, O my soul; all my inmost being,
PRAISE HIS HOLY NAME.
Praise the Lord, O my soul, and forget not all His benefits. Who forgives all your sins and heals all your diseases,
who redeems your life from the pit and crowns you with love and compassion.
Psalm 103:1-4

He will perfect that which concerns me.
Psalm 138: 8
OH LORD WHAT A LIST I HAVE.

Whatsoever things that are pure,
Whatsoever things that are lovely,
THINK ON THESE THINGS.
Phillipians 4:8

LEARN TO BE CONTENT
in whatever state I am.
Phillipians 4:11

LOVE NEVER FAILS.
1 Corinthians 13:8

238

"Food for the Soul"
CONTINUED

"MY SECRET TO STAYING YOUNG"
Who satisfies your desires with good things so that your youth
is renewed like the eagle's.
Psalm 103:5

FOR MY PRECIOUS PRAYER WARRIOR~ Elaina ~
What a servant of God. Mathew 28:1

We have to walk it out~ Ma Adams (Jesus is Ministries)

Annetta and Wesley Smith a family of music and prayer warriors. This family is so special to me and many others in our community. When they get together and sing "What a Day That Will Be." Makes us feel good about our future with our Jesus.

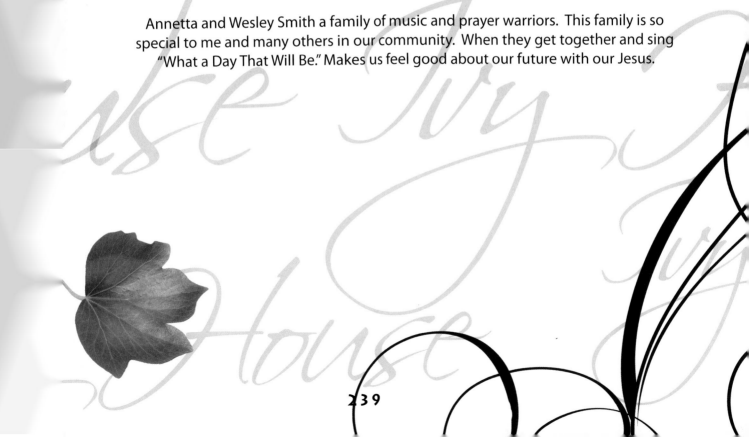

The Ivy House

...And I hope you
will get to come
eat with me today!